Nabokov's
Novels in Englis

Nabokov's Novels in English

Lucy Maddox

The University of Georgia Press
Athens

PS3527
A15
Z77
1983

Copyright © 1983 by the University of Georgia Press
Athens, Georgia 30602
All rights reserved

Designed by Design for Publishing, Bob Nance
Set in Mergenthaler VIP Palatino

The paper in this book meets the guidelines for permanence and
durability of the Committee on Production Guidelines for Book
Longevity of the Council on Library Resources.

Printed in the United States of America

Library of Congress Cataloging in Publication Data

Maddox, Lucy.
  Nabokov's novels in English.

  Includes index.
  1. Nabokov, Vladimir Vladimirovich, 1899–1977
—Style. I. Nabokov, Vladimir Vladimirovich, 1899–
1977. II. Title.
PS3527.A15Z77   813'.54   82-4893
ISBN 0-8203-0626-6   AACR2

for JIM

Contents

Acknowledgments

Acknowledgments are difficult because the number of people to whom one feels indebted is so large and because the final responsibility is so completely one's own. Of the many people who have assisted and encouraged this project in various ways, I would particularly like to thank my parents, James and Louise Bowers, for more kinds of support than I can adequately acknowledge; my colleagues Raymond H. Reno and Gay Gibson Cima, for consistently sound advice; and two very scrupulous and demanding readers, Anthony Winner and Michael Wood, for the kind of exactingness that is finally the best encouragement.

Editions Used

Ada or Ardor: A Family Chronicle. New York: McGraw-Hill, 1969.
Bend Sinister. New York: McGraw-Hill, 1973.
The Gift. Translated by Michael Scammell. New York: G. P. Putnam's Sons, 1963.
Glory. Translated by Dmitri Nabokov. New York: McGraw-Hill, 1971.
Lolita. New York: G. P. Putnam's Sons, 1955.
Look at the Harlequins! New York: McGraw-Hill, 1974. (Cited as *Harlequins*.)
Nabokov's Dozen. Garden City, N.Y.: Doubleday, 1958.
Nikolai Gogol. New York: New Directions, 1961. (Cited as *Gogol*.)
Pale Fire. New York: G. P. Putnam's Sons, 1962.
Pnin. London: Heinemann, 1957.
Poems and Problems. New York: McGraw-Hill, 1970.
The Real Life of Sebastian Knight. New York: New Directions, 1959. (Cited as *Knight*.)
A Russian Beauty and Other Stories. New York: McGraw-Hill, 1973.
Speak, Memory. New York: G. P. Putnam's Sons, 1966.
Strong Opinions. New York: McGraw-Hill, 1973.

Transparent Things. New York: McGraw-Hill, 1972.
The Waltz Invention. New York: Phaedra, 1966.

Anonymous. *The Song of Igor's Campaign.* Translated by Vladimir
    Nabokov. New York: McGraw-Hill, 1975. (Cited as *Song.*)
Pushkin, Aleksandr. *Eugene Onegin.* Translated, with commen-
    tary, by Vladimir Nabokov. Rev. ed. 4 vols. Princeton: Prince-
    ton University Press, 1975.

Nabokov's Novels in English

Introduction

The world inhabited by the characters in Nabokov's novels can be a maddening place, not because its processes seem random and meaningless, but because they give every indication of being carefully designed and carried out with meticulous attention to even the finest details. Coincidences, patterns, recurrences, and foreshadowings all seem to be reliable evidence of methodical, deliberate planning on the part of nature and fate. Nabokov's characters sense this "plexed artistry," as John Shade puts it in *Pale Fire*, and are predisposed to see in the turnings of their own lives evidence of the same manipulative will. The problem is that the intention behind the artistry is never revealed. In reviewing their lives, or in some cases others' lives, these characters begin with a puzzle that varies little from one novel to another: the reflected pattern of a life produces "a most melancholy and meaningful picture—but meaning what, what?" (*Ada*, p. 284). Nabokov's people are consistently frustrated by the sense of living on the edge of meaning, of being part of a complicated pattern that they get only glimpses of but that must surely make wonderful sense to someone, somewhere.

Among Nabokov's characters, John Shade comes closest to defining the attitude that lies behind the shape of the novels when he finds cause for "faint hope" in the conjecture that the design governing human fate may be, like the design of a complicated game, apparent only in retrospect:

> Yes! It suffices that I in life could find
> Some kind of link-and-bobolink, some kind
> Of correlated pattern in the game,
> Plexed artistry, and something of the same
> Pleasure in it as they who played it found.
> It did not matter who they were. No sound,
> No furtive light came from their involute
> Abode, but there they were, aloof and mute,
> Playing a game of worlds, promoting pawns
> To ivory unicorns and ebon fauns;
> Kindling a long life here, extinguishing
> A short one there; killing a Balkan king;
> Causing a chunk of ice formed on a high-
> Flying airplane to plummet from the sky
> And strike a farmer dead; hiding my keys,
> Glasses or pipe. Coordinating these
> Events and objects with remote events
> And vanished objects. Making ornaments
> Of accidents and possibilities. [*Pale Fire*, p. 63]

The kindling, extinguishing, and coordinating that give pleasure to Shade's unnameable manipulators duplicate the planned give-and-take of a game. They also suggest the process of artistic creation, and Shade goes on to exploit this similarity:

> The pen stops in mid-air, then swoops to bar
> A canceled sunset or restore a star,
> And thus it physically guides the phrase
> Toward faint daylight through the inky maze. [P. 64]

In the game of words, as in the game of worlds, the design necessarily changes as the game progresses, and the pattern of the whole cannot be evident until the last move is made or the last word written.

Nabokov's characters typically attempt to gain a perspective on the puzzling progress of their lives by writing about them (all of the eight novels in English are narrated in first person, and five are cast as personal memoirs), in the belief that imposing a narrative structure on the chaos of their experience will give the past the semblance of a carefully constructed novel and make the intentional pattern of the plot become clear. They are usually haunted by the ending of the narrative, which they know has already been written and filed away and will be appended later. They are concerned with finding the right way to read the beginning and middle so that the final scene, their own deaths, will seem a logical and just resolution to all that has come before. Yet, while the narrator writes in an effort to understand the fluid, multifarious (Nabokov might say "multicolored") course of his personal history, the artificial shapeliness of the narrative he produces betrays its distance from actual experience. The real conflict in a Nabokov novel, then, can be said to take place between the narrator and his narrative, and if there is a winner, it is the narrative.

In his last Russian novel, The Gift, Nabokov introduces a metaphor that is an apt figure for the sense of living in pursuit of an always fugitive meaning that troubles his characters and for the artificial structures they create in response. The metaphor comes from the dying poet Alexander Yakovlevich Chernyshevski, as he reflects on his past life and tries to find some rational relationship between it and his approaching death:

Of course I am dying. These pinchers behind and this steely pain are quite comprehensible. Death steals up from behind and grasps you by the sides. Funny that I have thought of death all my life, and if I have lived, have lived only in the margin of a book I have never been able to read. Now who was it? Oh, years ago in Kiev . . . Goodness, what was his name? Would take out a library book in a language he didn't know, make notes in it and leave it lying about so visitors would think: He knows Portuguese, Aramaic. Ich habe dasselbe getan. Happiness, sorrow—exclamation marks en marge, while the context is absolutely unknown. A fine affair. [P. 323]

Chernyshevski, on the verge of death, examines the import of his life and finds that he can reduce it to a single literary metaphor: all his experience adds up to no more than an accumulation of annotations to a text that remains unintelligible, even when the careful scholiast has made his final marginal comments.

John Shade uses a similar metaphor in *Pale Fire* when he suggests that it is possible to see *"Man's life as commentary to abstruse / Unfinished poem"* (p. 48). There is another interesting similarity between Chernyshevski and Shade. In his last lucid moment Chernyshevski reaches a conclusion about the possibility of life after death:

"What nonsense. Of course there is nothing afterwards." He sighed, listened to the trickling and drumming outside the window and repeated with extreme distinctness: "There is nothing. It is as clear as the fact that it is raining."

And meanwhile outside the spring sun was playing on the roof tiles, the sky was dreamy and cloudless, the tenant upstairs was watering the flowers on the edge of her balcony, and the water trickled down with a drumming sound. [P. 324]

John Shade, on the day of *his* death, reaches a quite different conclusion about the hereafter while speculating about his dead daughter:

I'm reasonably sure that we survive
And that my darling somewhere is alive,
As I am reasonably sure that I
Shall wake at six tomorrow, on July
The twenty-second, nineteen fifty-nine,
And that the day will probably be fine. [*Pale Fire*, p. 69]

Both poets need the consolation of certainty, whatever the ultimate answer may be; only uncertainty is finally unendurable. Yet in both cases Nabokov emphasizes the limitations on the individual's ability to know anything with certainty by positioning both poets beside a window, inside their own homes. What they see and hear from this accustomed and comfortable perspective ought to be the most familiar and reliable of impressions, and their very familiarity ought to provide emotional and intellectual comfort. But even this seemingly safe perspective is subject to distortion from the simple play of light and shadow, or from a neighbor lady's whims. Both Chernyshevski and Shade extrapolate from the familiar patterns of the world as they perceive it, reading backwards from their commentary to the given text. But both fail to take into account the deceptiveness—even deceitfulness—of nature and fate. It isn't raining outside Chernyshevski's window, and John Shade never wakes on July 22, 1959. In Nabokov's terms, the deceptiveness itself is evidence of intention and design; at the same time, it is a most effective way of keeping the design hidden, or keeping the text unreadable.

The verbal structures that Nabokov's narrators produce are also commentaries, attempts to explicate the mystifying text of personal experience and to locate and document the passages in it that might provide the key to the whole. The problem inherent in these attempts is suggested by two remarks Nabokov makes in his published interviews:

Reality is a very subjective affair. . . . You can get nearer and nearer, so to speak, to reality; but you never get near enough because reality is an infinite succession of steps, levels of perception, false bottoms, and hence unquenchable, unattainable. . . .
. . . I tend more and more to regard the objective existence of *all* events as a form of impure imagination—hence my inverted commas around "reality." Whatever the mind grasps, it does so with the assistance of creative fancy. [*Strong Opinions*, pp. 10–11, 154]

There is, of course, nothing very new about this kind of talk about the nature of the real; essentially the same attitude is implicit in Joyce, in Proust, even in James. What makes Nabokov's novels brilliantly innovative is exactly what made the fictions of Joyce, Proust, and James new: the way in which the subjective vision informs and determines the structure and style of the novel. In Nabokov's novels, the method of the commentary is an overt acknowledgment that the best that the poet, the novelist, the scholar, or the common reader can do is to make his private speculations about (on the subject of, and on the periphery of) the baffling text of "reality."[1]

The creative imagination is, in one sense, the villain in Nabokov's novels, since by its consistent meddling it succeeds in keeping his characters from ever confronting reality with the inverted commas removed. On the other hand, the imagination makes up for its treachery by making possible the creation of the other, more accessible world of fictional artifice. In writing their commentaries Nabokov's characters are of necessity victims of their own creative imaginations, so that what they produce is not, and cannot be—nor do they finally want it to be—a faithful record of past experience as it actually occurred. Memory and imagination work together to rearrange and recombine the actual into patterns and shapes that are more satisfying than the fragmentary shapes of the given world. The most vivid memories, Nabokov noted, are the result of "Mnemosyne's mysterious foresight in having stored up this or that element which the creative imagination may want to use when combining it with later recollections and inventions" (*Strong Opinions*, p. 78). In putting together their combinations Nabokov's narrators invent a new world which resembles but does not duplicate the one in which they have lived.

Clarification of the text is always one of the primary purposes of commentary; in writing about the past Nabokov's narrators are attempting to sort through the chaos of accumulated impressions and memories to find a locus of meaning in personal experience. Their commentary-art serves to bring experience into sharper focus by lifting it out of the range of two distracting nuisances—the "swarming in the eyes" which is space and the "singing in the ears" which is time (*Pale Fire*, p. 40)—and by bringing to bear on it the creative imagination, "that drop of water on a glass slide which gives distinctness and relief to the observed organism" (*Strong Opinions*, p. 154). But the re-created world of the imagination can have its sinister side as well; the most tortured of Nabokov's characters are those who fail to distinguish between the ideal images of imaginative art and the actual people and processes of ordinary life. These characters— Humbert Humbert is perhaps the clearest example—are haunted by images which never have belonged to the world of actuality, and never can. Humbert's obsession is with the image of a perfect nymphet, who is partly remembered, partly invented, and partly borrowed from an earlier poet's visions. His attempts to incarnate in Dolores Haze that impossible image, innocent in itself, make of him a madman and a moral monster. The creative imagination can clarify and animate the given world, but it can also breed monsters who make that world a hell for themselves and others.

There is an interesting passage in one of Nabokov's English short stories, " 'That in Aleppo Once . . .' " (published in *Nabokov's Dozen*), that illustrates beautifully and concisely this dual attitude toward the creative imagination. The story is in the form of a letter, written by a poet who has just fled Russia and addressed to another Russian writer who had emigrated earlier. The letter writer has a request to make of his friend: "I come to you like that gushing lady in Chekhov who was dying to be described" (p. 114). He is asking his friend to write a story about the narrator's experiences on his journey from Russia to America, in the belief that casting his experiences as a story will make sense of them. What he has to report seems at first a bizarre but plausible account of his wife's mysterious behavior during the journey and her eventual desertion; by the end of the story, however, it has become impossible to tell whether his wife ever existed at all or is simply an imaginative equivalent for the narrator's loneliness and sense of loss. The narrator describes leaving Russia with his bride, who, he says, in the course of their trip repeatedly disappeared and then reappeared, each time with a different account of where she had been, always teasing her husband's jealousy by sometimes affirming and sometimes denying that she had been with another man. The last time she disappeared the narrator searched for weeks before giving up hope and sailing from Marseilles alone. On board ship he encountered an old acquaintance who was shocked to hear that the narrator had sailed without his wife; "he looked taken aback and then said he had seen her a couple of days before going on board, namely in Marseilles, walking, rather aimlessly he thought, along the embankment" (p. 152).

The narrator recounts all this in his letter, written from New York, and concludes with his request:

Viewing the past graphically, I see our mangled romance en-
gulfed in a deep valley of mist between the crags of two matter-of-fact mountains: life had been real before, life will be real
from now on, I hope. Not tomorrow, though. Perhaps after tomorrow. You, happy mortal, with your lovely family (how is
Ines? how are the twins?) and your diversified work (how are
the lichens?), can hardly be expected to puzzle out my misfortune in terms of human communion, but you may clarify
things for me through the prism of your art.

Yet the pity of it. Curse your art, I am hideously unhappy. She
keeps walking to and fro where the brown nets are spread to
dry on the hot stone slabs and the dappled light of the water
plays on the side of a moored fishing boat. Somewhere, somehow, I have made some fatal mistake. There are tiny pale bits
of broken fish scales glistening here and there in the brown
meshes. It may all end in Aleppo if I am not careful. Spare me,
V: you would load your dice with an unbearable implication if
you took that for a title. [Pp. 152–153]

This narrator's "fatal" mistake is the same one that Humbert
Humbert makes, in that he wants to find in someone else's aesthetic vision those things that his lived experience has so completely failed to provide: clarification, consolation, certainty,
intensity—even if it must be the intensity of tragedy. In asking
his friend to tell a story, and in providing not only the plot but
some crucial images, he is really asking the writer to save his
life. Telling the story right could salvage the past and make the
future possible; conversely, telling the story in the wrong way
would surely mean death. If his friend uses "Aleppo" in the title,
that allusion to *Othello* would indicate that the pattern of his past
life so closely resembles the pattern of Othello's experience that
the only aesthetically satisfying way to complete the pattern is
with suicide—which the narrator is apparently already contemplating. On the other hand, the *Othello* allusion would give
his "hideously unhappy" life the force of tragedy and make of
him not only a victim, but a sympathetic and heroic one at that.
The narrator can well curse art, since its idealized images and
artificial structures have replaced for him the "matter-of-fact" reality that he found intolerably incomplete, inexplicable, and

painful. Reality has become for him a matter of literary allusion, and the result is, of course, madness. Like many others of Nabokov's characters, this narrator's need to know, to "fix" something once and for all, has become a fatal obsession. When that happens, as it so frequently does in Nabokov's fiction, the character's need for ultimate assurances, which he may allow his own imagination or someone else's to provide, can override his more enduring, but less compelling, need to feel morally comfortable in his world.[2]

While this narrator is typical of the many Nabokov characters for whom the siren song of the imagination makes the given world seem intolerably diminished, the story also contains a concise version of the answer that Nabokov's fictions consistently give to their own question: What can we make of a diminished thing? The "V" of the story, to whom the letter is addressed, has evidently found the three things that can make the world more than sufficient: ordinary, sublunary love ("how is Ines? how are the twins?"), the fascinating mysteries of nature ("how are the lichens?"), and the freedom to re-create the world imaginatively ("the prism of your art"). These things are worthy of the greatest human ardor, and they are enough to keep any man sane—even the creative artist—and to make of him a "happy mortal."

Nabokov's narrators are passionate annotators of reality, usually of their own private reality, who hope through "the alchemy of a scholium" (*Eugene Onegin*, 1:ix) to produce the key to the meaning of the whole. They keep diaries and notebooks and collect scraps of information to use in making their notes in the margin of the real. In putting these together, however, they are creating, with the aid of imagination, a new and artificial world, "constructing a mosaic out of genuine odds and ends with [their] own mortar" (*Song*, p. 12). The madmen in Nabokov's fiction move confusedly back and forth between the created and re-created worlds; his sane characters know that the re-created one, as splendid as it may be, is only an elaborately cross-referenced commentary on the meaning of the created one. But these sane characters also know that while artistic creation is essentially a form of compensation for the sense of incompleteness and the conviction of loss that are the inevitable results of hu-

man experience, this kind of compensation, rightly seen, can offer enormous pleasures. If what once seemed simple to us now
appears impossibly complex, we have the pleasure of recognizing that complexity can be far more interesting than simplicity. If
the answers that should be complete and obvious turn out to be
partial and elusive, we have still the pleasure of the pursuit, the
fascination of sorting through clues and anticipating resolu-
tions. And if the course of personal experience is consistently
unsatisfying, we have the pleasure of remaking it through the
imagination, and this time making it better. For Nabokov, this is
precisely what novelists do when they write novels, and what
readers do when they read them.

Any introduction to the general themes and methods of these
novels would be glaringly incomplete without some comment
on the one thing for which they are probably most well known
by every kind of reader—their luxuriant eroticism. It is no coincidence that the three best of these novels—*Lolita*, *Pale Fire*, and
Ada—are also the most sexually charged, or that in the least
effective of them, *The Real Life of Sebastian Knight*, the narrator
seems almost asexual. The eroticism of the books goes a long
way toward determining both their appeal and their success as
novels. Part of the reason is that frustrated sexual desire, as long
as it is someone else's, is always a potentially funny subject, one
which Nabokov is remarkably good at exploiting. This particular
combination of subject and method is sufficient to account for
much of the popular appeal of the novels; sex and humor, especially when handled as deftly as Nabokov handles them, can
guarantee readers. The importance of the eroticism to Nabokov's
themes and to his conception of character, however, requires
more explanation.

Taken in its largest context, the sexual desire of Nabokov's
narrators is a perfectly appropriate synecdoche for that compul-
sive need to possess the world beyond the self, to possess it sexually and intellectually, that is the real subject of the novels. The
sexual obsessions of many of these narrators are total, driven,
absorbing; the character at times runs entirely on sexual energy
and is willing to sacrifice everything else to his vertiginous,
often feverish sensuality. For him, the play of sunlight on a bare

arm, the fine hair on the back of a neck, or even the pattern of a vaccination scar can become the most heartbreakingly beautiful, mysterious, and tantalizing thing in the world. The sense of erotic vertigo can become almost frightening; Humbert Humbert, for instance, feels his very sanity threatened by the "rapture" of watching Lolita play her graceful game of tennis. The entire landscape of the character's world can become sex-drenched, as if it were sanctioning and encouraging his desire, so that words like *ardent*, *naked*, and *tender* appear frequently in his descriptions of the inanimate components of his world— trees, skies, and mountains. (Even in *Sebastian Knight* one of the key images of the book is that of a natural landscape animated by the sensual rhythm of human breathing, although significantly this image comes to us secondhand from Sebastian himself, and not from the seemingly bloodless narrator.)

Of all the narrators in the English novels, the one who seems least disoriented by the power of his own sexual desire is Van Veen, who is also the most athletic and indefatigable of Nabokov's lovers. Because he sees sexual possession as the one sure form of knowledge, Van is therefore led to interpret sexual lust as an instinctive defense against the potentially maddening multifariousness and transience of human experience.

It would not be sufficient to say that in his love-making with Ada he discovered the pang, the *ogon'*, the agony of supreme "reality." Reality, better say, lost the quotes it wore like claws— in a world where independent and original minds must cling to things or pull things apart in order to ward off madness or death (which is the master madness). For one spasm or two, he was safe. The new naked reality needed no tentacle or anchor; it lasted a moment, but could be repeated as often as he and she were physically able to make love. [*Ada*, p. 232]

The most obvious flaw in Van's philosophic approach is that it only intensifies the problem of frustration, both sexual and intellectual, since his analysis of the instant of reality he has isolated "shows a complex system of those subtle bridges which the senses traverse—laughing, embraced, throwing flowers in the air—between membrane and brain, and which always was and

is a form of memory, even at the moment of its perception"
(p. 233). If moments of reality are only synaptic, they are too
short-lived even to be apprehended intellectually, and can only
be recollected. The only real pleasures, it seems, are the ones we
have lost.

With the help of Ada's deflating common sense and his own
declining physical powers, Van eventually reconciles himself to
the obvious impossibility of living in a kind of orgasmic Eden
where one can fully possess not only the beloved but the whole
time-bound world as well. He settles instead for a much diminished but at least inhabitable place somewhere between heaven
and hell, where lust is sporadic but love endures anyway—the
familiar world of conventional marriage and shared old age. Van
is actually among the most fortunate of these narrators; of the
remaining seven, two end up in prison cells, one in a hospital
bed, and one, Charles Kinbote, may be alone in a remote mountain cabin but is more probably in a padded cell. The kind of
physical confinement these characters are driven into by the
frenzy of desire is emblematic of the ironic psychological course
that lust almost always takes in Nabokov's novels. The most vital
of his characters need to find their experience of the world, especially their erotic experience, not just satisfying but satiating;
when the external world fails them, their impulse is to turn
away from it and toward those inner landscapes and imaginatively recreated people that promise not to disappoint. The result
is a gradual disorientation and estrangement from the solid world
around them, and the states through which they pass may be
predictably pathological—mentally, socially, or even physically.

Nabokov's treatment of sexual desire in these novels is, then,
typically ambivalent. Some of the most stunningly effective and
moving writing in the books appears in those passages which
are the most purely erotic. The emotional and linguistic energy
of these passages convinces one of several things at once: of the
totally compelling nature of the narrator's sexual needs; of the
almost unearthly pleasure that sex can give him; and of Nabokov's sympathy with his narrator in both cases. On the other
hand, sexual pleasure is never simple in these novels, and sexual satisfaction is never complete. All of Nabokov's lovers are
troubled by their own version of the green serpent that inhabits

the Eden of Van and Ada's walled garden at Ardis. In their case, the serpent (as the text makes clear) is Lucette, the vulnerable child, whose eventual suicide is the result of Van and Ada's obsession with what they see as their completely innocent eroticism. In three other novels—*Bend Sinister*, *Lolita*, and *Pale Fire*—a child again serves as the most compelling representative of that world beyond the garden, in which mortality and morality are the enemies of desire, and in all three cases the child is again a sacrificial victim. The attractions of the garden are enormous, but in these novels Nabokov makes it clear that the fictional locations he gives it are the only possible ones he can envisage.

One

Pale Fire

Pale Fire is often considered the sport among Nabokov's novels and, depending on the reader's tastes, either dismissed as a genetic monster or hailed as an exciting new mutation. The proper place of *Pale Fire* among these novels, however, is not on the periphery but squarely in the center. Its departures from the other books—thematic and structural—are differences in degree only and not in kind. *Pale Fire* is the novel-as-commentary in its most audacious form, and it is in this regard the book to which the others point, in anticipation or in retrospect.

Pale Fire is also the most impressive and effective demonstration of the kind of tyrannical control that Nabokov exercises over his fictions. The narrator of this very complex novel, Charles Kinbote, sets out with a clear idea of what he intends to accomplish in his book: to annotate and explicate the long poem, apparently complete except for the final line, written by his friend John Shade. It is obviously true that Kinbote, even at the beginning, is not a disinterested scholar; he intends to explicate the poem according to his own lights, and so to demonstrate that the real, carefully camouflaged subject of the poem is actually Charles Kinbote himself. Given this rather large reservation, however, we can still take Kinbote at his word when he protests that he has "no desire to twist and batter an unambiguous *apparatus criticus* into the monstrous semblance of a novel" (p. 86). Kinbote would like, through judicious annotation, to *discover* himself enthroned and immortalized in Shade's poem, rather than having to *create* a place for himself there. But his commentary begins to slip out of his control, as Kinbote sees in his own words more interesting and promising possibilities than he finds in Shade's. He succumbs gradually and almost imperceptibly to the attractions of his own narrative and, in the process, to the requirements of the pattern of Nabokov's novel.

Kinbote's mad commentary on the poem is, in part, a deliciously comic parody of the kind of scholarly project that Nabokov himself undertook in his edition of Pushkin's *Eugene Onegin*, in which Nabokov's annotations are almost as eccentric, in their own way, as Kinbote's. But the parody in *Pale Fire* not only makes fun of scholarly arrogance and eccentricity; it also demonstrates that any commentary on a text, or even any close reading of a text, is necessarily going to result in distortion. That is, through the mad scholar Kinbote, Nabokov suggests that even the sanest reader will always be a subverter of the text he reads. The reasons for our own necessary misreadings are also suggested by Kinbote's exaggerated response to Shade's poem: we distort other people's texts in part because of our egocentricity, in part because of the obscurity of the writer's intentions (What should the last line of the poem be?), in part because our perceptions can be permanently skewed by someone else's earlier misreading (Kinbote's commentary, as mad as we know it to be, still changes the way we read Shade's poem). Most important—and here Nabokov's attitudes towards misreading seem most peculiarly, most eccentrically, his own—we consistently distort texts because, like Kinbote, we want those texts to do too much for us. Nabokov suggests that as readers we all have a lurking suspicion that if we could only find the right way to read texts, we would be safer, less anxious, less frightened. And if a first reading fails to provide the right answers, then we can reread with the assumption that the important agendas of the text are hidden, its significant messages are in code. If Nabokov is right about our desires as readers, then, what he has given us in *Pale Fire* may be just what we look for in all fiction—the comforting sense that the clues do lead somewhere and the code can be cracked.

Kinbote's first reading of Shade's poem distresses him because he cannot locate himself in its landscapes, either physical or psychological.[1] His old-world, baroque sensibility is baffled and offended by what he sees as the constrictive Americanness, the plainness, the "eminently Appalachian" (p. 296) quality of the poem; what he determines to discover on a second reading is the transforming magic, "that special rich streak of magical madness which I was sure would run through it and make it transcend its time" (p. 297). The kind of transforming magic that Kinbote then proceeds to supply, through the commentary, becomes an index to his own complex psychology and sensibility and to his particular obsession with meaning.

The most obvious source of the commentary is Kinbote's unremittingly energetic and inventive imagination; he has exactly the kind of imagination that he says the assassin Gradus lacks, the kind that is capable of contemplating "ghost consequences, comparable to the ghost toes of an amputee or to the fanning out of additional squares which a chess knight (that skip-space piece), standing on a marginal file, 'feels' in phantom extensions beyond the board, but which have no effect whatever on his real moves, on the real play" (p. 276). A second source of the commentary is Kinbote's agonizing sense of loss; while we are never exactly sure *what* he has lost, it is clear that he not only wants but needs to return to the past and reconstruct it, using the actual as raw material but rearranging it into shapes and patterns that are less painful and less frightening. Another recognizable impulse behind Kinbote's need to compensate for the inadequacy of the poem through the commentary is his insistent eroticism. He is one of the many Nabokovian characters capable of seeing most things in the world, even landscapes, as sexually charged, and since Shade, at least as a poet, is not one of those characters, Kinbote must infuse the poem with the sensuality that is an essential part of his "marvelous tale" (p. 296). Kinbote's eroticism becomes a synecdoche for a kind of sensual intelligence that is always potentially exhilarating, since it allows him to discover in nearly everything the possibilities for arousal, pleasure, and gratification of desire. At the same time, he is aware that his sensuality makes him even more of an alien in the American setting, since the sensualist is a distinctively un-American type and since among his American acquaintances eroticism is generally a subject for jokes. Through the commentary, then, Kinbote must somehow turn Shade's poem into a sacred text that will assure him that he is not an alien and a misfit everywhere, that the world beyond himself contains signs of his own personal significance, that somewhere there is a "refuge" for the "royal fugitive" (p. 81).

The novel raises a number of teasing questions about Kinbote's past without fully answering any of them. All we know for sure is that he is a sad, frightened, desperately lonely pederast who arrives in New Wye with an appointment to teach at Wordsmith University and a determination to impress his famous neighbor, Shade. (We can also be fairly sure that he has changed his name—his real one seems to be V. Botkin.) Part of his reason for wanting to ingratiate himself with Shade is simply that such an attachment would shore up his ego and his reputation. The more important reason is that he believes that Shade, as a poet, has a certain alchemistic power that might be used for Kinbote's own salvation—the capacity for "perceiving and transforming the world, taking it in and taking it apart, re-combining its elements in the very process of storing them up so as to produce at some unspecified date an organic miracle" (p. 27). The particular miracle Kinbote needs is the transformation of his own past into a tale of high romance and tragic heroism that would justify and ennoble his present terrified isolation. When Shade's poem fails to perform this specific miracle, Kinbote takes over the task himself in the commentary. He works in references to his childhood in the exotic kingdom of Zembla, then begins hinting that his was no ordinary childhood, then coyly confesses that he is in fact King Charles the Beloved of Zembla, exiled by revolution from his kingdom and hiding in New Wye from an "anti-Karlist" faction known as the Shadows and their chosen king killer, Gradus. In Kinbote's hands Shade's poem becomes a coded key to the wonders of an imagined world, a magic (Kinbote's word is "goedic") mirror reflecting back to Kinbote "echoes and spangles of my mind, a long ripplewake of my glory" (p. 297). Nabokov, in the course of his own long, at times Kinbotian commentary on *Eugene Onegin*, noted that "the pursuit of reminiscences may become a form of insanity on the scholiast's part" (2:32–33). Kinbote's pursuit of meaning in his past leads him into a shadowy kingdom of the imagination, where the miraculous possibilities that are hinted at in the "plexed artistry" of nature and visionary poems are realized in the actualities of everyday life.

Yeats's famous comment about Blake, that he was "a man crying out for a mythology, and trying to make one because he could not find one to his hand,"[2] is an appropriate description of a number of Nabokov's characters, most obviously Kinbote. But Kinbote has some very special requirements for his mythology. In the first place, as long as his mythology remains a purely private one, he cannot trust it to bear the emotional weight he has given it. The king must have his *scop* to tell his story; the poet must inspirit the heroes of the tale through his art before they can have an objective existence. "Once transmuted by you into poetry," Kinbote tells Shade, "the stuff *will* be true, and the people will come alive" (p. 214). Kinbote's belief in the literally life-giving and life-sustaining power of art is a function of his need to establish a satisfying version of his own identity. V. Botkin, American scholar of Russian descent, is (apparently) an ordinary, vulnerable, insignificant mortal. Charles Kinbote has the advantage over Botkin in that he at least knows he is actually an exiled king. His significance is assured—but even exiled kings are mortal and vulnerable, and their lives are in constant danger. Only King Charles has a chance for immortality and invulnerability; he can live on, safely preserved in art—like Shade's "gum-logged ant" (p. 41)—if only Kinbote can find an artist willing and able to reassemble his Zembla. He believes he has found that artist in Shade, the poet capable of transforming the world in a way that reminds Kinbote of the conjuror who could "turn his plate into a dove by tossing it up in the air" (p. 28). This is why Kinbote is so officiously persistent in telling Shade the Zemblan stories, and why possession of the finished poem is so crucial to him. With the note cards on which the poem is written distributed about his body, the exiled king is invulnerable, "plated with poetry, armored with rhymes, stout with another man's song, stiff with cardboard, bullet-proof at long last" (p. 300).

Kinbote's second requirement for his mythology is a corollary of the first: while it cannot remain private, it must be intensely personal. The epic saga of King Charles is to be simply a better way of telling the painful, shabby story of Charles Kinbote (or V. Botkin). Through his commentary, Kinbote intends to translate his private terrors and failures into the public story of the successes of calm, crafty Charles the Beloved. In his poem, Shade attempts a similar kind of translation, with the important difference that he proceeds in exactly the opposite direction:

> How ludicrous these efforts to translate
> Into one's private tongue a public fate! [P. 41]

Both men have suffered shocking losses, which leave them with unsettling questions about their own moral responsibility, and both respond by experimenting with interpretations of human experience that will make their losses and their fears more tolerable. Shade attempts to translate public fate into private significance; life and death become for him fascinating games of chance controlled by the unpredictable moves of some unidentifiable "they" who are "Playing a game of worlds" and "Making ornaments / Of accidents and possibilities" (p. 63). Kinbote, on the other hand, attempts to translate private fate into public significance; for him, personal failures are the result of carefully planned human conspiracies, and death is the relentlessly advancing assassin, Gradus. Both kinds of translation might be compared to the devising of a metaphor. In Kinbote's metaphor, however, the focal point is the vehicle rather than the tenor, and as the comparison is extended the vehicle assumes a more and more potent reality for him.

While it is absolutely necessary to Kinbote that his commentary reach a publisher and then a public audience, Shade's poem is obviously written for the private purpose of making

> Existence, or at least a minute part
> Of my existence

comprehensible to himself (p. 69). In a 1962 interview Nabokov commented that he did not think "an artist should bother about his audience. His best audience is the person he sees in his shaving mirror every morning" (*Strong Opinions*, p. 18). Shade ac-

knowledges that audience in canto 4 of his poem. In the course
of some rambling speculation about muses and the sources of
poetic inspiration, Shade describes the shaving mirror he has
rigged up in his bathtub and the daily ritual of shaving:

> And while the safety blade with scrape and screak
> Travels across the country of my cheek,
> Cars on the highway pass, and up the steep
> Incline big trucks around my jawbone creep,
> And now a silent liner docks, and now
> Sunglassers tour Beirut, and now I plough
> Old Zembla's fields where my gray stubble grows,
> And slaves make hay between my mouth and nose. [P. 67]

Shade whimsically and wittily reduces a traveler's map of the
world to the outlines of his own face; Kinbote, on the other
hand, attempts to impose his imprint on that map with all the
earnestness of one whose very life depends on the success of
the attempt. The justification Kinbote offers for his commentary
is that it will supply, ostensibly in the way of variant readings
and bits of Shade's biography, the "human reality" he feels is
missing from Shade's poem: "Let me state that without my notes
Shade's text simply has no human reality at all since the human
reality of such a poem as his (being too skittish and reticent for
an autobiographical work), with the omission of many pithy
lines carelessly rejected by him, has to depend entirely on the
reality of the author and his surroundings, attachments and so
forth, a reality that only my notes can provide" (pp. 28–29). As
it turns out, of course, the "attachments" Kinbote speaks of reduce to his own parasitic relationship to Shade, the biography
he supplies is King Charles's, and at least four of those valuable
"pithy" variants, Kinbote confesses in the index, are his own
contributions. One of these Kinbotian variants produces the
longest single entry in the commentary, the one detailing King
Charles's two trips down the secret passage from the palace to
the Royal Theatre. For Kinbote, "human reality" clearly means
whatever impinges on his own life.

The particular form that Kinbote's Zemblan fantasy takes can
be largely accounted for by his need to assign an acceptable pub-

lic cause—a murder plot—to his irrational fears. He cannot tolerate the idea of the "chaos of chance" (p. 226) as the determinant of fate in this life or the next; hence his vaguely Christian belief in a God who is "the Judge of life, and the Designer of death" (p. 225) and his insistence that what might appear to be paranoid terror is actually justifiable wariness of the anti-Karlist Shadows stalking him. The Zemblan story also accounts for his acute loneliness; an exiled king must expect to be alone with his secret knowledge and his memories of former adulation and affection. Another very useful benefit of Kinbote's fantasy is that it allows him to legitimize his homosexuality, to explain it as one of the "manly Zemblan customs" (p. 208) which had come to be traditional among monarchs in that remote, exotic country whose mores one might well expect to differ from those of a small town in upstate New York. As for the land of Zembla itself, Kinbote has not created it ex nihilo; the geography of *Pale Fire* includes a real Zembla with a real king who was deposed by revolution shortly before Kinbote's arrival in New Wye, and whose fate is a matter of speculation. The form of the private Zemblan fantasy is therefore largely determined by a chance concatenation of public events.

The evolution of Kinbote's delusion is very similar to the case of the civil clerk in "The Diary of a Madman" by Gogol—a writer Nabokov admired, appropriately, for understanding that "great literature skirts the irrational" (*Gogol*, p. 140). The intolerable ordinariness and poverty of his life push Gogol's clerk to the edge of the abyss of madness; he remains there until a political development in Spain entices him over the edge by providing a convenient and comfortable place for him to land:

December 5: I read the newspapers all morning. Strange things are happening in Spain. . . . They write that the throne has been vacated and that the ranking grandees are having difficulty in selecting an heir. . . . It's impossible that there should be no king. There must be a king but he's hidden away somewhere in anonymity. It's even possible that he's around but is being forced to remain in hiding for family reasons or for fear of some neighboring country such as France. Or there may be other reasons.

Year 2000, April 43: This is a day of great jubilation. Spain has a king. They've found him. *I* am the King. I discovered it today. It all came to me in a flash. It's incredible to me now that I could have imagined that I was a civil-service clerk. How could such a crazy idea have entered my head?[3]

Kinbote and Gogol's clerk both seize the opportunity of a political disruption to stage their own private revolutions. Both find a conveniently assumable identity in a missing king. More important, both arrive at the exhilarating but disorienting conclusion that personal identity can be rejected like an unpopular king, and that replacing it is only a matter of discovering the alternative self that is hidden away somewhere in anonymity, fully formed, waiting to be found, named, and empowered. The identity of the self, in other words, does not have to be created gradually through accretion; instead, it can be discovered—in a flash—in the text of a newspaper, or someone else's poem.

Kinbote actually finds considerable encouragement in New Wye for exchanging his identity for that of King Charles:

Pictures of the King had not infrequently appeared in America during the first months of the Zemblan Revolution. Every now and then some busybody on the campus with a retentive memory, or one of the clubwomen who were always after Shade and his eccentric friend, used to ask me with the inane meaningfulness adopted in such cases if anybody had told me how much I resembled that unfortunate monarch. I would counter with something on the lines of "all Chinese look alike" and change the subject. [Pp. 264–65]

While no one in New Wye thinks that Kinbote really is King Charles, despite the "inane meaningfulness" he hears in their remarks, it seems clear that his resemblance to the king is great enough to plant the seeds of a "brilliant invention" (p. 238), as Shade calls it, in his mind. Kinbote's decision to become the king may well have been clinched by the visiting German lecturer's insistence (among a group of Kinbote's colleagues gathered in the Faculty Club, including his archenemy Gerald Emerald and his idol John Shade) that the resemblance between Kinbote and the missing king is so close as to be "absolutely unheard of" (p. 265).

The general outline of Kinbote's fantasy is provided for him, then, by his particular needs and by the happy circumstance that he looks very much like a king who dropped out of sight at a convenient moment. To fill in that outline Kinbote draws on a number of sources, holding up to his goedic mirror bits and pieces culled from his experience and his reading and transforming them into the elements of a "wild glorious romance" (p. 296). Several of the major characters in the Zemblan fantasy are recognizable as back-formations from flesh-and-blood people among Kinbote's acquaintances. The despised Gerald Emerald, for example, becomes the despised Izumrudov, "one of the greater Shadows" (p. 255).[4] Kinbote can say of Izumrudov what he cannot freely say of his acerbic and aggressively heterosexual young colleague Emerald, much as he would like to: "He was a merry, perhaps over-merry, fellow, in a green velvet jacket. Nobody liked him, but he certainly had a keen mind. . . . How one hates such men!" (p. 256). Gordon Krummholz, the "musical prodigy" (p. 200) whom Gradus meets at Lex and whom Kinbote lustfully describes as a "young woodwose" (p. 201) with hair a tint lighter than his nectarine skin, is a metamorphosed member of the Wordsmith faculty, "Assistant Professor Misha Gordon, a red-haired musician" (p. 216). The anti-Karlist Shadows are clearly the collective incarnation of the vague irrational sources of Kinbote's terror. In order to describe them, however, Kinbote reaches into his recent New Wye experiences and comes up with, first, the stories he has heard of revenge threats against the life of his landlord, Judge Goldsworth, and second, two advertisements he found preserved in the scrapbook of Shade's bizarre Aunt Maude. The first is an ad for the Talon Trouser Fastener; the second, an ad for the Hanes Fig Leaf Brief, depicts a "modern Eve worshipfully peeping from behind a potted tree of knowledge at a leering young Adam in rather ordinary but clean underwear, with the front of his advertised brief conspicuously and completely shaded" (p. 115). Kinbote is *not* amused at these advertisements which treat "the mysteries of the male sex" with flippancy and make "disgusting mischief in sacrosanct places" (p. 115). Here is Kinbote's description of the Shadows: "Spiteful

thugs! They may be compared to hoodlums who itch to torture
the invulnerable gentleman whose testimony clapped them in
prison for life. Such convicts have been known to go berserk at
the thought that their elusive victim whose very testicles they
crave to twist and tear with their talons, is sitting at a pergola
feast on a sunny island or fondling some pretty young creature
between his knees in serene security—and laughing at them!"
(pp. 149–50). The Zemblan fantasy allows Kinbote to bypass
ordinary social restraints and give free expression to a swarm of
intense private feelings: hatred for the taunting Gerald Emerald,
lust for Misha Gordon (among others), the fears that accompany
his sexual inversion, and horror at the thought of death.

Some of the elements of the Zemblan story seem designed to
assure that it will "transcend its time" and endure as a work of
art. But Kinbote, as he himself admits, is an imitator and adaptor,
not an original thinker; he must borrow from proven sources.
For example, the story of the king's flight from Onhava through
the mountains is embellished with the matter of fairy tales: the
"gnarled farmer and his plump wife who, like personages in an
old tedious tale offered the drenched fugitive a welcome shelter"
and gave him "a fairy-tale meal of bread and cheese, and a bowl
of mountain mead" (p. 140). Kinbote also includes echoes of one
of the hoariest of all sources, *Hamlet*, but only after holding the
play up to his goedic mirror. After Queen Blenda's death the
young Prince Charles is tormented by "the strong ghost" of his
mother (p. 111), who encourages him from beyond the grave to
marry the Ophelia-like Fleur de Fyler. Kinbote ends the note describing the failure of this "chaste romance" with an account of
the lynching of "two baffled tourists from Denmark" (p. 112)—
Rosencrantz and Guildenstern?—who were mistaken for the
arsonists who set fire to the Exposition of Glass Animals in
Onhava. (Given Nabokov's description of *Hamlet* as "the wild
dream of a neurotic scholar" [*Gogol*, p. 140], these allusions
seem particularly appropriate for Charles Kinbote.)

Kinbote also fleshes out his narrative with assorted bits taken
directly from Shade's poem. The "clockwork toy" that Shade
keeps as a reminder of his first brush with death, for example,
becomes the "clockwork man" Gradus, the agent of death. The
curious interest of Mr. Campbell, young Charles's tutor, in book

mites and bear hunting seems less curious when we recognize
that it is derived from Shade's description of the curriculum at
the Institute of Preparation for the Hereafter, which emphasized

> Precautions to be taken in the case
> Of freak reincarnation: what to do
> On suddenly discovering that you
> Are now a young and vulnerable toad
> Plump in the middle of a busy road,
> Or a bear cub beneath a burning pine,
> Or a book mite in a revived divine. [P. 54]

Kinbote's commentary details two journeys: the flight of
Charles from Onhava to New Wye and the progress of Gradus
by the same route to the same destination. Both journeys ultimately fail in their objectives. Gradus comes to New Wye seeking to kill the king and kills the poet instead. The king comes to
New Wye seeking a pastoral refuge (Kinbote several times refers
to New Wye as "Arcady"), but finds that "even in Arcady am I,
says death in the tombal scripture" (p. 174). The progress of
King Charles from faraway Onhava (the name means "far away"
in Zemblan) through the perilous and mysterious Bera Mountains and finally to his new Arcadia is, on one level, a progress
through a variety of experimental postures, an attempt on Kinbote's part to borrow a prefabricated vision that will allow him to
escape the prison of his identity and the terrifying knowledge of
his mortality. Kinbote's borrowing is, of course, selective, since
his particular needs require a perspective that will give his perceptions the authenticity of truth, allow him to see his freakish-
ness as heroic individualism, and grant him the luxury of imaginative transcendence.

In one particularly revealing passage which purports to be a
comment on the suicide of Shade's daughter, Hazel, Kinbote
suddenly lapses into the vocabulary of an inept plagiarist who
has been dipping into the odes of Keats and Wordsworth. Kinbote begins with a strained admission of his own temptation to
"get it over with, this business of life" (p. 219) and then continues with a lyrical outburst of borrowed sentiment:

If I were a poet I would certainly make an ode to the sweet urge to close one's eyes and surrender utterly unto the perfect safety of wooed death. Ecstatically one forefeels the vastness of the Divine Embrace enfolding one's liberated spirit, the warm bath of physical dissolution, the universal unknown engulfing the minuscule unknown that had been the only real part of one's temporary personality.

When the soul adores Him Who guides it through mortal life, when it distinguishes His sign at every turn of the trail, painted on the boulder and notched in the fir trunk, when every page in the book of one's personal fate bears His water-mark, how can one doubt that He will also preserve us through all eternity? [Pp. 221–22]

The abrupt change of voice which will mark the final sentence in this note is a good indication that all the ecstasy and consolation that came before were simply lifted from an anthology to serve the needs of the moment: "We who burrow in filth every day may be forgiven perhaps the one sin that ends all sins." It is also interesting to note that the New Wye which Kinbote hopes will be a new refuge for him suggests a convenient comparison with the Wye River of Wordsworth's "Tintern Abbey," and that the word *Tintern* lurks suspiciously in the name of Zembla's highest mountain, Mount Glitterntin. Moreover, Kinbote the exiled king descends from the blue (literally, by parachute) into his strange new country, translating into parodic actuality Wordsworth's metaphor in the "Intimations" ode of the child who comes from afar, "trailing clouds of glory," an exile from "that imperial palace whence he came."

The "wild glorious romance" that Kinbote believes Shade is writing for him is as necessary as his own tentative poses, for reasons which are suggested by Nabokov's discussion of literary romanticism in the *Eugene Onegin* commentary. There Nabokov defines a romantic epic as one "in which the tragic and the comic, the lofty and the lowly, the sacred and the profane, the metaphysical generalization and the physical detail, and so forth are pleasingly mingled" (3:35). An epic of this sort, especially one written by a sympathetic poet capable of "perceiving and transforming the world," would surely have the scope to encompass the extremes of the Zemblan material. The formal strategies of such a romance could provide a way of translating one man's psychological conflicts into archetypal, dialectical patterns of universal human experience. Kinbote himself suggests the outlines for this dialectical structure: "Whereas an objective historian associates a romantic and noble glamor with Karlism," he writes, "its shadow group must strike one as something definitely Gothic and nasty" (p. 150).

No wonder, then, that Kinbote is shattered to find that Shade's *Pale Fire* is not a "kind of *romaunt* about the King of Zembla" but "an autobiographical, eminently Appalachian, rather old-fashioned narrative in a neo-Popian prosodic style" (p. 296). In order to salvage his king and his epic, Kinbote must remake the poem through the commentary, taking apart its elements and recombining them with himself at their center, finding in the impersonality of Shade's words all the intensity and complexity of his very private world. To this end, Kinbote works out a justification for the enormous liberties he has to take with Shade's poem. "A few written signs," he says, are capable of containing "immortal imagery, involutions of thought, new worlds with live people, speaking, weeping, laughing." But it requires a "true artist" to decode those signs and release their magic, revealing "the web of the world, and the warp and the weft of that web" (p. 289). In addition to his decoding, Kinbote as scholiast-artist must also add those valuable variants that will seduce readers of his edition of *Pale Fire* into believing that his interpretation—his decoding—is not eccentric or subversive.

Kinbote's conclusion that it is the "warp and weft" of the web of the world that finally matters is a resolution forced on him by the failure of Shade's poem to live up to his expectations. His metaphor is very much like the one Shade chooses to describe the similar resolution he reaches at the end of canto 3 of his poem. Shade's resolution also grows out of an initial disappointment. He recounts reading a newspaper article about someone who had an experience precisely parallel to his: a heart attack, a few moments of "death" before the heart resumes beating, and a vision during those moments of "a tall white fountain" (p. 59). The two appearances of that fountain Shade sees as "a signpost and a mark" (p. 61), convincing objective proof of a world beyond the grave. When Shade discovers that the "fountain" he read about was a misprint for "mountain," his reaction is exactly like Kinbote's reaction to the poem: shattering disappointment, then a resolution that makes a virtue of the necessity of confronting this disturbing trick that language has played on him:

> Life Everlasting—based on a misprint!
> I mused as I drove homeward: take the hint,
> And stop investigating my abyss?
> But all at once it dawned on me that *this*
> Was the real point, the contrapuntal theme;
> Just this: not text, but texture; not the dream
> But topsy-turvical coincidence,
> Not flimsy nonsense, but a web of sense.
> Yes! It sufficed that I in life could find
> Some kind of link-and-bobolink, some kind
> Of correlated pattern in the game,
> Plexed artistry, and something of the same
> Pleasure in it as they who played it found. [Pp. 62–63]

Shade's web metaphor illustrates a perspective that characterizes his thinking throughout, both in the poem and in his comments as Kinbote records them. Shade extrapolates from the intricate patterns of the web of the world to his own life. The "plexed artistry" of the outer, visible world is everywhere evident; to be a sensitive observer of that world, as Shade is, is to recognize that "we are most artistically caged" (p. 37). The highly symmetrical, balanced artifice of *Pale Fire*'s rhymed couplets is perfectly suited to Shade's sensibility and aesthetic vision:

> Maybe my sensual love for the *consonne*
> *D'appui*, Echo's fey child, is based upon
> A feeling of fantastically planned,
> Richly rhymed life.
>   I feel I understand
> Existence, or at least a minute part
> Of my existence, only through my art,
> In terms of combinational delight;

And if my private universe scans right,
So does the verse of galaxies divine
Which I suspect is an iambic line. [Pp. 68–69]

In commenting on the incongruity between the dishevelment of Shade's physical appearance and the harmony of his inner life, Kinbote remarks that Shade "was his own cancellation" (p. 26). Kinbote's remark is ironically apropos in other ways as well. In the first place, Shade finds evidence of universal design in "topsy-turvical coincidence," yet his own death is the result of a coincidence—his chance resemblance to Judge Goldsworth. Paradoxically, the sensibility that allows for life everlasting based on a misprint must also allow for death based on mistaken identity. Second, Shade values the symmetry of art because it appears to him fundamentally mimetic; his balanced couplets and cantos reflect for him a universal harmony that extends to the life of the individual. Yet Shade does not live to finish the final couplet, and that missing final line, by radically altering the imitating form, must by implication radically alter the perception of the thing imitated. The grounds of Shade's "faint hope" include the cancellation of the hope.

Kinbote's web metaphor, on the other hand, is a justification of his solipsism; the strands of the world's web—the warp and the weft—have been (he is convinced) spun out intentionally to entangle him. Kinbote concludes that one must look at the "underside of the weave" to understand that the pattern of fate, which seems impersonal, is cunningly plotted. In his commentary he has a look at the underside of Shade's poem and finds himself, "the beholder and only begetter, whose own past intercoils there with the fate of the innocent author" (p. 17). But—like Shade—Kinbote has laboriously constructed a trap for himself. His purpose in writing the commentary was to discover and solidify an acceptable identity for himself through another man's life and art, to translate that man's art into signs and symbols of his own personal significance. That Kinbote believes he has done, in spite of Shade's failure to cooperate: "Here and there I discovered in it and especially, especially in the invaluable variants, echoes and spangles of my mind, a long ripplewake of my glory. . . . My commentary to this poem, now in the

hands of my readers, represents an attempt to sort out those
echoes and wavelets of fire, and pale phosphorescent hints, and
all the many subliminal debts to me" (p. 297). The commentary
is a goedic mirror, transforming another man's autobiographical
poem into the coded story of Kinbote's glorious and purely
imaginary past. And if judicious decoding worked once, it can
work again:

I shall continue to exist. I may assume other disguises, other
forms, but I shall try to exist. I may turn up yet, on another
campus, as an old, happy, healthy, heterosexual Russian, a
writer in exile, sans fame, sans future, sans audience, sans
anything but his art. . . . Oh, I may do many things! History
permitting, I may sail back to my recovered kingdom, and with
a great sob greet the gray coastline and the gleam of a roof in
the rain. [Pp. 300–301]

Kinbote has found the way to escape a sad, sordid, and lonely
life through his magic mirror. But the trap is laid, for the mirror
has been signed from the other side by Gradus. He will be there,
a "bigger, more respectable, more competent Gradus" (p. 301),
no matter how often the story is changed. To see the coded story
of one's life in all things is also to see there a coded message of
death, written by Sudarg of Bokay.

It is always tempting to see Nabokov's paired characters (Kinbote and Shade, Humbert and Quilty, Van and Ada) as opposing
sides of a single, divided self, and to read the novels in which
the paired characters appear as attempts to fuse this divided self
into a psychological whole.[5] In *Pale Fire* it is especially tempting
to see Shade's detached, thoughtful objectivity and Kinbote's
rash, intense subjectivity as the two poles of the artistic personality, perhaps even of Nabokov's own personality. Nabokov's
interest, however, is not in psychological reconciliation; the attributes of his paired characters are, instead, distillations of irreconcilable ways of viewing the world and the self. The public
event and the private response to it, the objective fact and the
subjective feeling, the outer and inner realities, the text and the

commentary, make equally convincing claims as the place to begin the search for significance. In Nabokov's terms, one of the chief values of art is that because it is fundamentally metaphoric it is able to speak of two things at once, to juxtapose the irreconcilable inner and outer realities in a single vision, as *Pale Fire* juxtaposes Shade's poem and Kinbote's commentary. (The novels which present these paired perspectives also make clear the dangerous extremes to which each kind of perspective can lead: Kinbote's intense subjectivity, for instance, leads to self-destructive madness, as Clare Quilty's sterile objectivity in *Lolita* leads him to the passionless destruction of others.)

Nabokov's successful experiment in sustaining this metaphor-like double perspective throughout an entire novel, and incorporating both perspectives into a single comprehensive vision, suggests Joyce's similar method in *Ulysses*—a book Nabokov knew well and alluded to frequently (usually a Nabokovian form of high praise). Joyce uses the Leopold Bloom-Stephen Dedalus opposition, as Nabokov uses the Kinbote-Shade opposition, as the basis of a kind of stereoscopic vision that is shaped by the structure of the novel itself. A more interesting and rewarding comparison, however, can be made between *Pale Fire* and another work to which it frequently alludes, Boswell's *Life of Johnson*. In fact, the nature of the Kinbote-Shade relationship strongly suggests that Nabokov intentionally modeled it on the Boswell-Johnson relationship: in both cases the insecure and unsettled younger man attaches himself to the older, established literary figure, not only looking to him for direction but eventually seeing in him the agent of the disciple's own fame and even immortality. Shade remarks at one point that he has been told he resembles Samuel Johnson, and Kinbote reinforces that suggestion of similarity in the descriptions of his "misshapen" idol, whose ungainly physical appearance "was so little in keeping with the harmonies hiving in the man, that one felt inclined to dismiss it as a coarse disguise or passing fashion" (pp. 24–25). At times Kinbote lapses into recognizably Boswellian accounts of his conversations with Shade, and in these passages Shade's mannerisms and his speech, which takes a sudden, surprising epigrammatic turn, become caricatures of Johnson's:

"Nay, sir," (said Shade, refolding a leg and slightly rolling in his armchair as wont to dǫ when about to deliver a pronouncement) "there is no resemblance at all. I have seen the King in newsreels, and there is no resemblance. Resemblances are the shadows of differences. Different people see different similarities and similar differences."   . . .
     Shade (smiling and massaging my knee): "Kings do not die—they only disappear, eh, Charles?" [Pp. 265–66]

(Compare Boswell's observation of Johnson that "while talking or musing as he sat in his chair, he commonly held his head to one side towards his right shoulder, and shook it in a tremulous manner, moving his body backwards and forwards, and rubbing his left knee in the same direction," or his mention of Johnson's habit of "rolling himself about in a strange ridiculous manner." [6])
     Both Boswell and Kinbote set out to provide their subjects with what Kinbote calls "human reality." Both succeed—but, ironically, they succeed in spite of their avowed intentions to be strictly objective. It is significant and appropriate that the book originally published as The Life of Samuel Johnson, LL.D., by James Boswell, is known to modern readers as Boswell's Life of Johnson. The genius, the appeal, the "human reality" of the biography, and of Kinbote's commentary, are due not to the author's objectivity but to the massive infusion of his own personality and style into the narrative. At the beginning of his book Boswell promises the reader that Johnson "will be seen as he actually was";[7] what he then provides is something very different but perhaps even better—Johnson's life as registered by the fascinating mind of Boswell.
     At one point Boswell records a Johnsonian apothegm that is particularly appropriate to Pale Fire: "Modern writers," Johnson remarked, "are the moons of literature; they shine with reflected light, with light borrowed from the ancients."[8] A similar image of the reflecting moon appears in the passage in Shakespeare's Timon of Athens from which John Shade takes the title of his poem:

> The sun's a thief, and with his great attraction
> Robs the vast sea; the moon's an arrant thief,

And her pale fire she snatches from the sun;
The sea's a thief, whose liquid surge resolves
The moon into salt tears.* [4.3.439–43]

Boswell's narrative and Johnson's life borrow their light and their vitality from each other—as do Kinbote's commentary and Shade's poem. The vision of *Pale Fire* is finally compounded of both perspectives, and its particular quality depends upon the interplay of the two.

There are other significant literary pairings or oppositions in *Pale Fire*, the most obvious of which is found in the names of Judge Goldsworth and Wordsmith University. In splitting apart and then reassembling the names of Goldsmith and Words-worth, Nabokov suggests the sort of eclectic perspective—the sort that would, perhaps, allow one to read Goldsmith and Wordsworth in an interlinear edition—that he requires of the readers of *Pale Fire* but denies to its characters.

The resolution that is inherent in the structure of *Pale Fire* is the same one that Humbert Humbert reaches at the end of *Lolita*. Humbert recognizes that his nymphet and his child are both "real" but that they can never be fused in a *single* reality. At the same time, these discrete, irreconcilable realities are capable of enriching, animating, and illuminating each other; each borrows and reflects a "pale fire" from the other. Humbert loves his child because she reflects the imagined nymphet, and he adores his nymphet because she partakes of the real child. The division of *Pale Fire* into Shade's poem and Kinbote's commentary offers a structural equivalent of the kind of double vision that Humbert eventually acquires. The novel provides its own evidence that neither perspective is thoroughly reliable or accurate: the end result of Shade's reasoned argument is a shaky truce with fate and the mistaken conclusion that he will be alive on July 22, while

---

*Kinbote offers his own version of this passage, which he re-Englishes from a Zemblan translation; in the process, he characteristically confuses some sexual identities:

> The sun is a thief: she lures the sea
> and robs it. The moon is a thief:
> he steals his silvery light from the sun.
> The sea is a thief: it dissolves the moon. [P. 80]

Kinbote's imaginative restructuring of the personal past brings him to the equally mistaken conclusion that Shade's killer is the Zemblan assassin, Gradus. Neither man, however, is entirely wrong. Shade is right in assuming that there is no *logical* reason for him to die on the twenty-first, as Kinbote is right in believing that the man standing at his door is a killer. A close approach to the truth requires both perspectives, both ways of reasoning about the self and the world. Yet, even that kind of double vision is finally too limited to anticipate or account for the great surprise—the madman who is Death, waiting on the wrong doorstep to kill the wrong man.

Two

The Real Life of Sebastian Knight

Pale Fire, published in 1962, and Nabokov's first novel in English, *The Real Life of Sebastian Knight*, written more than twenty years earlier, are similar in ways that Nabokov called attention to in his last book, *Look at the Harlequins!* There the narrator (a burlesque Nabokov) describes a novel he has written entitled *See under Real*. The novel, an amalgamation of *Sebastian Knight* and *Pale Fire*, is the fictional biography of a brilliant writer who has just died, written by a charlatan critic named Hamlet Godman, and edited by the writer's brother. As the book progresses, the editor's footnote comments begin to encroach more and more on the pages of text, until finally "in the course of the last chapters the commentary not only replaced the entire text but finally swelled to boldface" (p. 121). In both *Sebastian Knight* and *Pale Fire* the narrator's sole avowed purpose is to provide a commentary—in the first case on the life and works of a successful novelist, and in the second on a single work by a well-known poet; in both the commentary quickly subsumes its original subject as the commentator becomes more obsessed, altering the original when he needs to and filling in its gaps with his own imaginings.

Both narrators (as well as the editor-brother of *See under Real*) show a distinct family likeness to yet another narrator, the character K in an unfinished novel which Nabokov abandoned in 1940, one year after he finished *Sebastian Knight*. The first two chapters of that novel, written in Russian and provisionally titled *Solus Rex*, were later translated by Nabokov and published in *A Russian Beauty and Other Stories* as "Ultima Thule" and "Solus Rex." K, a recent widower,[1] is an artist who has been commissioned to do a series of illustrations for an epic poem about the legendary king of a remote island country. Since the poem is written in a Scandinavian language K cannot read, he knows only the bare outlines of the plot and must supply the rest from his imagination. In the prefatory note to "Ultima Thule" Nabokov says of K that "in the course of evolving an imaginary country (which at first merely diverted him from his grief, but then grew into a self-contained artistic obsession), the widower becomes so engrossed in Thule that the latter starts to develop its own reality" (p. 147).

While K is more recognizably kin to Charles Kinbote in *Pale Fire* than to V in *Sebastian Knight* (Kinbote even suggests *Solus Rex* as a title for John Shade's poem), the three are alike in that all are betrayed by the sheer creative energy of their own imaginations. They choose to become, in effect, citizens of a country of the mind, a place over which they assume they will have absolute control, but which eventually declares its independence of them. For both Kinbote and V the autonomous energy of the imagination eventually becomes fatally disorienting; both conclude their commentaries (K was not permitted to conclude his) with cryptic passages in which they appear to have relinquished all sense of themselves as discrete, physical beings with distinct personalities.[2] V abruptly announces that "Sebastian's mask clings to my face, the likeness will not be washed off. I am Sebastian, or Sebastian is I, or perhaps we both are someone whom neither of us knows" (p. 205). Kinbote's valedictory suggests that he too will now change masks: "I shall continue to exist. I may assume other disguises, other forms, but I shall try to exist" (*Pale Fire*, p. 300).

V's disorientation is, as his confusing book demonstrates, a gradual process which goes through three distinct phases: his actual contacts with the living Sebastian, his researches into the past after Sebastian is dead, and finally the composition of his book about Sebastian, in which he attempts to consolidate what he has learned in the first two phases into an explanation of the meaning of Sebastian's life. Sebastian alive merely puzzles V and piques his curiosity; Sebastian dead turns his curiosity into an absorbing fascination, and by the time he begins to write, his book has become the record of a "self-contained artistic obsession" that blinds him to the perceptions of truth which his narrative contains. V's obsession with his half-brother's life begins with an episode which is not recorded until the end of the book, when V rushes to the dying Sebastian's bedside only to find that he has arrived too late.[3] V has explained earlier that he made that desperate trip because he was "so sure that if I could find a dying man alive and conscious I would learn something which no human being had yet learnt" (p. 76). He has arrived at this assurance partly through a dream in which Sebastian appears to him and tells him something of "absolute moment" (p. 190), and partly through reading Sebastian's last novel, *The Doubtful Asphodel*. In that book a dying man, randomly recalling images from his past, suddenly finds those images fusing in a dramatic flash of insight into the meaning of all things:

The answer to all questions of life and death, "the absolute solution" was written all over the world he had known: it was like a traveller realising that the wild country he surveys is not an accidental assembly of natural phenomena, but the page in a book where these mountains and forests, and fields, and rivers are disposed in such a way as to form a coherent sentence. . . . Thus the traveller spells the landscape and its sense is disclosed, and likewise, the intricate pattern of human life turns out to be monogrammatic, now quite clear to the inner eye disentangling the interwoven letters. And the word, the meaning which appears is astounding in its simplicity. . . . Now the puzzle was solved. [Pp. 178–79]

The man dies, leaving the miraculous word unspoken, and V becomes convinced that the dying Sebastian must also know the secret and will reveal it to him if he can only reach him in time. Missing Sebastian, V determines to re-create his life in the belief that by following the course of Sebastian's life and thought he can collect those images that were breaking like waves on the dying man's consciousness and discover the secret that Sebastian surely knew.

V's quest is doomed to failure from the beginning, for reasons which his own narrative makes clear but which V himself never recognizes. There is one moment in the novel when V seems very close to attaining the emotional and intellectual sympathy with Sebastian that would allow him to penetrate the mysteries of his half-brother's life. It occurs when V arrives at the hospital where Sebastian is lying ill and is permitted to sit for a while out-side the sick man's room:

His presence in the next room, the faint sound of breathing, gave me a sense of security, of peace, of wonderful relaxation. And as I sat there and listened, and clasped my hands, I thought of all the years that had passed, of our short, rare meetings and I knew that now, as soon as he could listen to me, I should tell him that whether he liked it or not I would never be far from him any more. The strange dream I had had, the belief in some momentous truth he would impart to me before dying—now seemed vague, abstract, as if it had been drowned in some warm flow of simpler, more human emotion, in the wave of love I felt for the man who was sleeping beyond that half-opened door. How had we managed to drift apart? . . . How little I knew of his life! But now I was learning some-thing every instant. That door standing slightly ajar was the best link imaginable. The gentle breathing was telling me more of Sebastian than I had ever known before. If I could have smoked, my happiness would have been perfect. A spring clanked in the couch as I shifted my position slightly, and I was afraid that it might have disturbed his sleep. But no: the soft sound was there, following a thin trail which seemed to skirt time itself, now dipping into a hollow, now appearing again,— steadily travelling across a landscape formed of the symbols of silence—darkness, and curtains, and a glow of blue light at my elbow. [Pp. 202–3]

The lulling sentimentality of this moment is abruptly under-cut by the revelation of its great irony: the sick man in the bed is not Sebastian after all. Sebastian is already dead, and V has been brought, through a nurse's error, to the room of a perfect stranger.

The error that has led V to rhapsodize over a stranger's breathing is neither so cruel a trick on the part of fate, nor so high-handed a move on Nabokov's part, as it might seem. The moment in the hospital has awakened in V a "simpler, more human emotion" than he has ever felt for Sebastian before, a sympathy that is even stronger than his obsession with finding out who Sebastian really was and what he knew. V's unguarded emotional response to the sound of a sleeping stranger's breathing underscores a point which the narrative makes clear to the reader, but which V never understands: that the real Sebastian is and will always be a stranger, a shadowy memory whose secrets will remain unspoken.

In his description of the dying man's moment of revelation Sebastian used the metaphor of a traveler who "spells the landscape" and finds that the world can be read as a coherent, meaningful sentence. V also uses the metaphor of a landscape in his description of the man's breathing, but his metaphor is, unknown to him, much closer to the mark than Sebastian's. The landscape of Sebastian's metaphor contains emblems that are the components of significant speech; V's landscape, on the other hand, is "formed of the symbols of silence." Because he wants so desperately to believe in the saving power of the dying man's word, V fails to recognize that it is his own silent, unexpressed emotions that have brought him closest to a sympathetic understanding of Sebastian. V's narrative belies his own intentions for it by affirming that the most appropriate and compelling image of "real life" is a purely sensuous one: the irregular sound of human breathing, crossing a patterned but silent landscape. Sebastian's "real life"—like all reality, no matter how intensely its presence and its meaning may be felt—is silent at the center.

The hospital scene, which comes at the end of the book, is from the reader's point of view a fitting resolution to V's story of frustrated attempts to reconstruct and convert into language the real life of Sebastian Knight. From V's perspective, however, it is the point at which his quest really begins. V leaves the stranger's bedside determined to write a biography that will account for all that Sebastian was and thought and felt: this time he will not miss Sebastian. His book begins, therefore, where V assumes such a biography should begin: "Sebastian Knight was born on the thirty-first of December, 1899, in the former capital of my country" (p. 5). What follows is at once the record of his researches into Sebastian's life and an acknowledgment of his failure to uncover any remarkable secrets that would lead him closer to the "absolute solution."

In the course of his researches V discovers that he has been beaten to the draw as Sebastian's biographer by a Mr. Goodman, Sebastian's former secretary, who has dashed off his *The Tragedy of Sebastian Knight* in an attempt to take best advantage of the market for a book about a man still fresh in his grave. Goodman is an obvious charlatan, an example of those critics Nabokov has described as "belonging to the good old school of 'projected biography,' who examine an author's work, which they do not understand, through the prism of his life, which they do not know." [4] In the Nabokovian catalogue of possible authorial sins, Goodman's most heinous one is his attempt to make his commentary sociologically and politically relevant. Believing that a biography ought to be written "from a special point of view which would make the subject fascinating" (p. 59), Goodman portrays Sebastian as a product and victim of the post–World War I era, "a youth of acute sensibility in a cruel cold world" (p. 62), and then condemns him for his aloofness "in an age when a perplexed humanity eagerly turns to its writers and thinkers, and demands of them attention to, if not the cure of, its woes and wounds" (p. 117). Mr. Goodman's second unpardonable sin is stupidity. He writes in clichés, makes factual errors, and is apparently too obtuse to recognize Sebastian's jokes. For example, he includes in his book an account of a novel Sebastian says he wrote and then destroyed. That novel, Sebastian told him, "was about a fat young student who travels home to find his mother married to his uncle; this uncle, an ear-specialist, had murdered the student's father" (p. 64). Mr. Goodman, V notes, misses the joke. In Goodman Nabokov paints—with very broad strokes—a satiric portrait of the literary hanger-on, the pompous critic who writes ex cathedra about matters he is incapable of understanding. His presence in this book, however, seems almost gratuitous, and we are not sorry when V, having mounted his attack on Goodman's biography, abruptly dismisses it: "I shall not refer any more to Goodman's book. It is abolished" (p. 119).

In the course of his researches V makes mistakes of his own which grow directly out of his obsession with discovering the "absolute solution" that he believes Sebastian found. In the first place, V errs in believing that a human life is an unbroken stream and that by following the windings of that stream one can fully understand the "real" life of another. Early in the book V admits to a wish that his subject were a fictional character, since then he "could have hoped to keep the reader instructed and entertained by picturing my hero's smooth development from infancy to youth"* (p. 20). Later, having discovered that Sebastian had a passionate, disastrous affair with a woman whose identity he does not know, V determines that finding this woman is "a scientific necessity," that she is "the missing link in his evolution" (p. 120). Failing in his first attempt to learn her identity, V considers abandoning his project: "The stream of the biography on which I longed so to start, was, at one of its last bends, enshrouded in pale mist; like the valley I was contemplating. Could I leave it thus and write the book all the same? A book with a blind spot. An unfinished picture,—uncoloured limbs of the martyr with the arrows in his side" (p. 125).

Because V cannot rest content with an unfinished picture, and because he needs to collect those images the dying man saw, he begins to fill in the gaps in his knowledge of Sebastian's life with images of his own creation. He envisions Sebastian on solitary bicycle rides at Cambridge; he imagines Sebastian and Clare Bishop's idyllic life together in London; he provides an elaborate picture of Clare on a day she spends alone waiting for Sebastian—even supplying the details of the weather. V tips his hand at one point when he describes, in three separate, lush vignettes, his purely imaginary version of Sebastian's meetings with his first

*Compare V's notions about "smooth development" with the last stanza of Nabokov's poem "We So Firmly Believed" (1938). The "you" of the poem is identified as "my youth":

> You've long ceased to be I. You're an outline—the hero
> of any first chapter; yet how long we believed
> that there was no break in the way from the damp dell
> to the alpine heath. [*Poems and Problems*, p. 89]

youthful love, Natasha Rosanov. Since V did not know Natasha as a girl he cannot envision her clearly, so he must create her to finish the picture, gradually filling in her outline and even coloring her limbs. He first imagines Sebastian and Natasha in a boat: "A girl is sitting at the helm, but we shall let her remain achromatic: a mere outline, a white shape not filled in with colour by the artist" (p. 138). In the second and third scenes the picture of Natasha starts to become clearer: "The painter has not yet filled in the white space except for a thin sunburnt arm streaked from wrist to elbow along its outer side with glistening down. . . . The seated girl's shape remains blank except for the arm and a thin brown hand toying with a bicycle pump" (pp. 138–39). V is gradually turning the Natasha-abstraction into an image, so that he can close one more of those unbearable gaps in his picture of Sebastian's life.

In a passage describing Sebastian's prose style, V unwittingly but very neatly defines the problems he is creating for himself by giving his imagination a free hand with Sebastian's past: "I cannot even copy his manner because the manner of his prose was the manner of his thinking and that was a dazzling succession of gaps; and you cannot ape a gap because you are bound to fill it in somehow or other—and blot it out in the process" (p. 35). V in effect attempts to mimic Sebastian's memory, not realizing that memory itself is a succession of gaps and not a continuum, that the whole, "real" life of Sebastian Knight will remain elusive. Sebastian's friends and his lovers are, as V says of the characters in *The Doubtful Asphodel*, "but commentaries to the main subject" (p. 174)—and like those characters, they are as likely to lead the seeker away from the main subject as toward it. In comparing Sebastian's first love affair with his last, V stumbles on a truth that a less obsessed man would surely have taken to heart: "Two modes of his life question each other and the answer is his life itself, and that is the nearest one can approach a human truth" (p. 137).

Nabokov's Russian novelette *The Eye* (*Soglyadatay*, 1930) describes an investigation very much like V's into the defining secrets of the self (Nabokov is much more apt to use the word *soul*, perhaps to avoid any psychoanalytic implications), but there are relevant differences between the two books. In *The Eye* the protagonist Smurov's quarry is himself, and his pursuit leads him to precisely that conclusion about the identity of the self that V's narrative unsuccessfully pushes him toward. Smurov painfully scrutinizes himself and discovers a bewildering variety of images of Smurov, but no type, no original model: "For I do not exist: there exist but the thousands of mirrors that reflect me. With every acquaintance I make, the population of phantoms resembling me increases. Somewhere they live, somewhere they multiply. I alone do not exist. Smurov, however, will live on for a long time" (p. 113). The paradox that Smurov sees clearly is exactly the basis of V's confusion. Sebastian's phantoms will live for a long time—as long as there are people who remember him or read his books—but the definable, unchangeable, "real" Sebastian simply does not exist.

V notes that the technique of one of Sebastian's books, *Success*, is based on the "fundamental assumption that an author is able to discover anything he may want to know about his characters, such capacity being limited only by the manner and purpose of his selection in so far as it ought to be not a haphazard jumble of worthless details but a definite and methodical quest" (p. 95). V begins his own quest to discover the real life of Sebastian Knight methodically enough; he begins it, in fact, ab ovo, by recording on the first page of his book an entry from the diary of a certain Olga Olegovna Orlova (V notes the "egglike alliteration" of her name) describing the weather on the day of Sebastian's birth. Immediately following this description, however, V indulges in a long parenthetical aside on the inability of the old woman's diary entry to compete with spontaneous memory in capturing the reality of a typical December day in Russia:

Her dry account cannot convey to the untravelled reader the implied delights of a winter day such as she describes in St. Petersburg; the pure luxury of a cloudless sky designed not to warm the flesh, but solely to please the eye; the sheen of sledge-cuts on the hard-beaten snow of spacious streets with a tawny tinge about the middle tracks due to a rich mixture of horse-dung; the brightly coloured bunch of toy-balloons hawked by an aproned pedlar; the soft curve of a cupola, its gold dimmed by the bloom of powdery frost; the birch trees in

the public gardens, every tiniest twig outlined in white; the
rasp and tinkle of winter traffic . . . and by the way how queer
it is when you look at an old picture postcard (like the one I
have placed on my desk to keep the child of memory amused
for a moment) to consider the haphazard way Russian cabs had
of turning whenever they liked, anywhere and anyhow, so that
instead of the straight, self-conscious stream of modern traffic
one sees—on this painted photograph—a dream-wide street
with droshkies all awry under incredibly blue skies, which, farther away, melt automatically into a pink flush of mnemonic
banality. [Pp. 5–6]

The past as V recalls it here is a collection of random sensory
impressions, freely combined into a single image. The force of
this composite image, and the contrast between the "dream-wide
street with droshkies all awry" of the past and the "straight, self-
conscious stream of modern traffic" should have alerted V to the
impossibility of his attempt to bring the past to life by simply
arranging verifiable events in sequential order. Here as elsewhere, V and his own narrative have become adversaries; while
he continues his "definite and methodical" quest for the reality
of the past, his narrative affirms that the only meaningful record
of the past is to be found in the "haphazard jumble of worthless
details" that memory preserves. (Sebastian's significant-looking
birth date, December 31, 1899—the last day of a century—is itself one indication of what is wrong with V's whole procedure.
There is a slight asymmetry, an imperfect fit, between the cate-
gories and taxonomies used to impose an arbitrary order on historical time and the kinds of measurements that apply to the
time of the personal past.)

V's second mistake, also the result of his obsession, is in assuming that it is possible to follow the course of an author's life
by following the course of his books. If V were an artist himself,
he would know that books do not contain real lives. (In his commentary to *Eugene Onegin* [2:5] Nabokov dismisses those mis-
readers who "search for 'real life' in the dead ends of art.") V
confesses that while he knows very little of Sebastian's life,
he knows the books "as well as if I had written them myself"
(p. 203). As he encounters more and more obstacles in his quest

and as he becomes increasingly convinced that Sebastian is "laughingly alive in five volumes" (p. 52) and nowhere else, V resorts to those volumes more often for help in his quest. In his obsession with finding the man behind the author V begins to people his own world with characters from Sebastian's books, especially those who appear in the dying man's visions in *The Doubtful Asphodel*. The chess player Schwartz, the fat Bohemian woman, the attentive plainclothes man, the lovely tall primadonna, the sobbing old man being comforted by a girl in mourning, and the Swiss scientist who shoots his mistress and then himself have all appeared in the course of V's researches. (Only one of these characters, the "pale wretch noisily denouncing the policy of oppression" [p. 175], either does not appear or is too cleverly hidden for this reader to find him.)[5]

In addition to these, two characters from Sebastian's earlier books also put in appearances, both of them coming to V's rescue when he has reached a seeming impasse. Mr. Siller, a character in one of Sebastian's short stories whom V describes as "perhaps the most alive of Sebastian's creatures" (p. 104), turns up as the German salesman Mr. Silbermann, offering his aid—which turns out to be invaluable—at the moment when V is most in despair over the prospect of finding Sebastian's mysterious Russian mistress. The other character who reappears in slightly altered form is the conjuror from Sebastian's novel *Success*. The passage that V quotes from that novel contains the following exchange between the conjuror, who is wearing underwear that reveals his calves, and another character named William: "William sat down on the bed and said: 'You ought to dye your hair.' 'I'm more bald than gray,' said the conjuror. . . . He folded his trousers with care. . . . 'I am merely happy,' said William. 'You don't look it,' said the solemn old man. 'May I buy you a rabbit?' asked William. 'I'll hire one when necessary,' the conjuror replied" (pp. 99–100).

After Mr. Silbermann has helped V to identify Sebastian's Russian mistress as Nina Rechnoy, V goes to her address and finds there a Madame Lecerf, who professes to be a friend of Nina's and promises to arrange a meeting for V. She invites V to her country house, where she serves him rabbit for lunch. Joining them for this lunch is "a rather handsome man in plus-fours with a solemn face and a queer grey streak in his fair sparse hair," who is silent throughout the meal. Afterwards, "the blond gentleman carefully folded his napkin" and withdrew (p. 167). This strange silent man, who turns out to be Russian, later performs a conjuring feat of his own, when he helps V trick Madame Lecerf into revealing that she is actually Nina Rechnoy, the missing link V has been searching for.

By the end of V's account the world of his actual experience and the world of Sebastian's fiction (on the day he finishes writing *Success* Sebastian announces, "I have finished building a world, and this is my Sabbath rest" [p. 90]) have become so inextricably intertwined that neither V nor the reader can hope to untangle them. V himself says of his quest that "I sometimes cannot help believing that it had gradually grown into a dream" but that nevertheless "I am forced to recognize that I was being led right" (p. 137). While we recognize the reasons for V's obsession and the stages by which the real becomes more illusory for him and illusion more real, we are still left with an unanswerable question: By whom is V being "led right"? By the shade of Sebastian, trying, as V believes, "in some unobtrusive way . . . to be helpful" (p. 101)? Or has Sebastian been so successful in creating a world that his characters have sprung into life and are helping V along? Or is it the conjuror Nabokov who is leading V and the reader further into the carnival-mirror world of his art that, like a dream, uses "the pattern of reality for the weaving of its own fancies" (p. 137)?

V never discovers the dying man's secret, but he does learn another one, "namely: that the soul is but a manner of being— not a constant state—that any soul may be yours, if you find and follow its undulations. The hereafter may be the full ability of consciously living in any chosen soul, in any number of souls, all of them unconscious of their interchangeable burden. Thus— I am Sebastian Knight" (pp. 204–5). V's hermetic secret is not very enlightening. Has Sebastian chosen to live in V's soul, among others? Has V followed the undulations of Sebastian's soul so closely that he has now convinced himself that he is Sebastian? Or is it the conjuror-author again, speaking through his creature as the curtain comes down, giving notice to the audience that there will be other performances, that he will claim other souls by following their undulations through the span of a book? One feels the same frustration on finishing this book as V feels on finishing *The Doubtful Asphodel*: the book ends before the clarifying word is spoken, and "we hold a dead book in our hands" (p. 180).

I began this chapter by pointing out the structural and thematic similarities between *Sebastian Knight* and *Pale Fire*. While these similarities are clear, there is one very important difference between the two novels that is equally clear: *Pale Fire* is a dazzling success, and *Sebastian Knight* is a perplexing failure. The problems the book poses for the reader are the same ones that troubled readers of Sebastian Knight's novels. At one point V discusses Sebastian's books with a business acquaintance who thinks Sebastian is an intellectual snob. "Asked to explain, he added that Knight seemed to him to be constantly playing some game of his own invention, without telling his partners its rules" (p. 181). Nabokov has said enough about his own aesthetic premises for us to suspect that this character is in fact giving Sebastian's art a backhanded compliment. In one published interview, for example, Nabokov compared the creation of "worthwhile art" to the composition of a chess problem, explaining that both are characterized by inventiveness, complexity, and "splendid insincerity" (*Strong Opinions*, p. 161). Charles Kinbote also plays a complex, inventive game of his own devising, but we are able to discern the rules as the game progresses, to discover the reasons for Kinbote's unreliability as a narrator, and to delight in watching the evolution of the web of fantasy and illusion that Kinbote spins out around himself.

Pale Fire provides the kind of touchstone—John Shade's poem —that is missing from *Sebastian Knight*. Since we know as little about Sebastian's life as V does, and less than V knows about his work, V's unreliability as a narrator becomes disconcerting and confusing. For instance, all we know about Sebastian's books we learn from V and the few passages he quotes from them. Yet we have to doubt V's astuteness as a literary critic, since we learn that he was "hypnotised" by the "perfect glory" of a short story— sent to him as part of a mail-order writing course—which concerned "a wicked Chinaman who snarled, a brave girl with hazel eyes and a big quiet fellow whose knuckles turned white when someone really annoyed him" (p. 35). We also have ample reason to doubt V's qualifications as the biographer of his half-brother. He is, for example, very defensive about his and Sebastian's Russian origins, insisting rather stuffily that "Sebastian was brought up in an atmosphere of intellectual refinement, blending the spiritual grace of a Russian household with the very best treasures of European culture" (p. 13), and that Sebastian's "somewhat artificial" passion for England "could not, I am sure, exclude real affection for the country where he had been born and bred" (p. 27). Sebastian, on the other hand, drops his Russian surname in favor of his mother's English name, speaks and writes only English after he leaves Russia, and is annoyed and embarrassed when he finds that his Cambridge tutor knows he is Russian.

V has at least one other shortcoming as Sebastian's biographer. Sebastian has three important love affairs during his life, all of them described and interpreted by V. Yet V himself is puzzlingly obtuse and squeamish about sexual matters: the "very sound of the word 'sex' with its hissing vulgarity and the 'ks, ks' catcall at the end" seems "inane" to him (p. 105); he characterizes virtually all the women he meets as types; he admires Clare Bishop (who has cropped hair and large, knuckly hands) for the masculine quality of her imagination; and he is appalled to find himself momentarily tempted to make love to the attractive and seductive Nina Rechnoy, concluding that "I was losing my grip somehow" (p. 168). These limitations make us hesitant to accept V's various deductions and conclusions as accurate—but then we have little else to go on. His commentary is baffling because we cannot know when it is a response to the "main subject" and when it has veered away from that subject and is simply being propelled by its own momentum.

V himself admits that Sebastian's last book, *The Doubtful Asphodel*, leaves him perplexed: "I sometimes feel when I turn the pages of Sebastian's masterpiece that the 'absolute solution' is there, somewhere, concealed in some passage I have read too hastily, or that it is intertwined with other words whose familiar guise deceived me" (p. 180). Readers of *Pale Fire* must surely feel that the clue to the hiding place of the Zemblan crown jewels is also there somewhere, that one more careful reading will turn it up. But the search for the crown jewels is a game we don't really mind losing, because it is so clearly only a game. In *Sebastian Knight*, on the other hand, the pieces missing from the book's mosaic are crucial. Perhaps Nabokov intended for us to finish his book with the same haunting suspicion that V has on finishing Sebastian's book; that is, if Nabokov's book mirrors Sebastian's book which in turn mirrors the way life itself teases those who believe in an absolute solution that can be systematically sought out, then Nabokov has succeeded—but it is a Pyrrhic victory. Charles Kinbote's commentary delights us because it *does* use the pattern of reality for the weaving of its own enchanting fancies; and Charles Kinbote, incidentally, is an enchanting character. V, on the other hand, is a humorless, dull character, and it is impossible to distinguish either the pattern of the reality he comments on or the final pattern of his commentary. We do, ultimately, hold a dead book in our hands.[6]

Three

Bend Sinister

Nabokov's novels are always about art, and the intrusive presence of the author keeps reminding us of the necessarily artificial nature of the text we are reading. This combination of art-consciousness and self-consciousness in the novels makes them seem at once distinctively modern and curiously old-fashioned. What the novels consistently say about literature is that—Henry James be damned—the only reason for its existence is that it does *not* attempt to represent life. Nabokov's insistence on the insincerity and artificiality of art, and the impressionistic vocabulary in which he makes that insistence, bear a strong resemblance to the familiar theories of the fin de siècle English aesthetes, especially Oscar Wilde. Nabokov was aware enough of the similarity to raise the matter himself so that he could discourage the comparison; rather than admiring Wilde, he professed to dislike him for his hypocrisy and timidity, dismissing him as one of those "dainty poets" who were actually "rank moralists and didacticists" (*Strong Opinions*, p. 33).

Nabokov's art and Wilde's *are* in the end quite different; what they share is an intense antipathy toward what Wilde calls "the prison-house of realism"—the kind of art that attempts to imitate, and pass judgment on, things as they really are at a given historical moment.[1] Both Nabokov and Wilde, for instance, disliked Henry James, and regretted in similar terms the waste of his skill as a stylist in the service of a dull attempt at verisimilitude:

My feelings toward James are rather complicated. I really dislike him intensely but now and then the figure in the phrase, the turn of the epithet, the screw of an absurd adverb, cause me a kind of electric tingle.[2]

Mr. Henry James writes fiction as if it were a painful duty, and wastes upon mean motives and imperceptible "points of view" his neat literary style, his felicitous phrases, his swift and caustic satire.[3]

In his insistence that "what makes a work of fiction safe from larvae and rust is not its social importance but its art, only its art" (*Strong Opinions*, p. 33), Nabokov is, like Wilde, at the farthest possible remove from the kind of realist who insists that it is the honesty of the artist which most affects the reader. In fact, the differences between James and Nabokov appear greatest when each speaks of the responsibility of the novelist to his audience and to his fictions. In his essay on Trollope, for example, James is appalled by Trollope's wanton and "suicidal" delight in violating the illusion of reality—of historical reality—by "reminding the reader that the story he was telling was only after all, a make-believe. He habitually referred to the work in hand (in the course of that work) as a novel, and to himself as a novelist, and was fond of letting the reader know that this novelist could direct the course of events according to his pleasure." For James, the real problem with these authorial intrusions is that they are "inartistic," since their effect is to destroy the created impression of life which is the entire raison d'être of the novel. In short, while Nabokov strongly implies that there is no necessary distinction between artifice and artistry, James implies just as strongly that acknowledging the artifice is fatal to the art.[4]

Nabokov's objection to realistic fiction, however, was not as vociferous as Wilde's, nor were the grounds of his argument with it as extreme. Where Wilde, for instance, considered art to be "absolutely indifferent to fact,"[5] Nabokov insisted that the creative artist must

study carefully the works of his rivals, including the Almighty. He must possess the inborn capacity not only of recombining but of re-creating the given world. In order to do this adequately, avoiding duplication of labor, the artist should *know* the given world. Imagination without knowledge leads no farther than the back yard of primitive art, the child's scrawl on the fence, and the crank's message in the market place. Art is never simple. . . . Art at its greatest is fantastically deceitful and complex. [*Strong Opinions*, pp. 32–33]

Nabokov's quarrel was not, as Wilde's was, with the attitude that fiction should say something truthful, but with what he saw as the regimentation and oversimplification of truth in fiction.

We cannot know to what extent Nabokov's attitudes toward the right purpose of literature were the natural result of his particular sensibility, and to what extent they were shaped in reaction to the events taking place in Russia during the early part of the century—the years when Nabokov was training himself to become a writer. At any rate, it is not surprising that a Russian-born writer who loved prerevolutionary Russia and despised Soviet Russia as much as Nabokov did (or who lost as much because of the transformation) would also despise the kind of literature that the new government demanded from its writers. Like most other Russian émigrés, Nabokov for years held out the hope that he could return to his homeland to continue the career he was being forced to pursue in the artificial atmosphere of émigré life—the career of a Russian writer. Those hopes were gradually dimmed, however, by the increasing repressiveness of the Soviet regime and especially by the kind of regimentation that was being successfully imposed on the arts. The First Congress of Soviet Writers, held in 1934, was the occasion for the announcement of a formal doctrine that had been in effect unofficially for years. That doctrine, apparently put together by Stalin and Maxim Gorky (whom Nabokov disliked intensely), denounced such experimental writers as Andrey Biely and Alexander Blok, both of whom Nabokov admired, as "formalists" who were undermining the great tradition of Russian realism. That tradition was to be continued under the Soviets, the doctrine declared, but now it was to be turned to the purpose of affirming the social order, rather than criticizing it.[6]

Bend Sinister, the first novel Nabokov wrote after coming to America, can be seen as his most direct fictional response to both the new Russian government and the new Soviet realism. The most self-consciously artificial of his novels in English, *Bend Sinister* is an indictment of the common impulse Nabokov saw behind both political totalitarianism and the misguided tendency of writers or readers to inflict "general ideas" on works of art. Both are, in Nabokov's view, ways of avoiding the need to confront and comprehend complexity; both are evidence of the fear of—or the inability to understand—ambiguity, skepticism, and eccentricity, either intellectual or aesthetic. The ruling party of the dictatorship in *Bend Sinister*, for example, is the Party of the Average Man, and its manifesto calls for a general leveling of human consciousness, on the principle that universal happiness is not possible "so long as there [exist] some individuals with more brains or guts than others" (p. 75). Similarly, the dictatorship spawns and encourages the kind of literary critic who finds that the real theme of *Hamlet* is "the corruption of civil and military life in Denmark. . . . Consciously or unconsciously, the author of *Hamlet* has created the tragedy of the masses and thus has founded the sovereignty of society over the individual" (p. 108).

Nabokov clearly intended that the eccentric form of this novel, with its shifting narrative stance, its authorial intrusions, and its extraordinary ending, should make the efforts of his fictional dictator to bully people and works of art into conformity with the commonplace appear ironically foolish and ineffectual. In drawing the parallel, however, Nabokov worked himself into a difficult situation which was finally impossible to get out of. In the first place, the indictment of tyranny in *Bend Sinister* would seem to make of the novel precisely the kind of art that Nabokov is in the process of condemning: a political novel with social intent. Nabokov attempted to escape that dilemma in part through the ending of the book, when the narrator intrudes and disavows all that has come before, and in part by providing some explanatory comments in the introduction (added in 1963):

The story in *Bend Sinister* is not really about life and death in a grotesque police state. My characters are not "types," not carriers of this or that "idea." Paduk, the abject dictator and Krug's former schoolmate (regularly tormented by the boys, regularly caressed by the school janitor); Doctor Alexander, the government's agent; the ineffable Hustav; icy Crystalsen and hapless Kolokololiteishchikov; the three Bachofen sisters; the farcical policeman Mac; the brutal and imbecile soldiers—all of them are only absurd mirages, illusions oppressive to Krug during his brief spell of being, but harmlessly fading away when I dismiss the cast. [Pp. vii–viii]

The ending and the introductory comments, however, do not get rid of the dilemma; in fact, they help to point up the real crux of the problem. Having depicted a brutal police state that is reminiscent of actual totalitarian regimes of the recent past (Nabokov has even incorporated into the book parts of Lenin's speeches and a section of the Soviet constitution) and having worked strongly and deliberately on the reader's sympathies in describing the atrocities committed by the rulers of that state, Nabokov then dismisses the whole sinister business as a fiction. The difficulty, of course, is that real dictatorships are not plays on words or absurd mirages that will go away when we stop thinking about them. By denying that his novel can have any social or political import, Nabokov has also had to deny it any lasting value as art. *Bend Sinister* in effect declares its own inability, as a work of art, to come to terms with the irrefutable reality of the least aesthetically pleasing of all things—willful human cruelty.[7]

The narrator's ploy at the end of *Bend Sinister* is an egregious instance of a technique that Nabokov has used (usually to better advantage) many other times. Howard Nemerov has said of Nabokov that "his subject is always the inner insanity and how it may oddly match or fail to match the outer absurdity, and this problem he sees as susceptible only of *artistic* solutions."[8] The endings of the novels make it clear, however, that solution and resolution are not the same thing. In only three of the novels in English, *Lolita*, *Ada*, and *Look at the Harlequins!*, does the character within whose mind the conflict plays itself out arrive at a satisfactory resolution of that conflict, and the resolution always comes in the character's acknowledgment that inner and outer are finally reconcilable only in the fantasies of art. The other novels settle for a solution, a deus ex machina which extricates the character from his difficulties while the novel collapses around him. The characters in these novels are obsessed with meaning; they make intolerable demands on their world and its creator by attempting to understand the puzzle of their own identities—to find personal significance in their impersonal world—and to make sense of that greatest of all absurdities, death. For these novels Nabokov provides a solution-ending that is both an answer and an evasion. These endings announce that the revels now are ended, the actors melted into thin air, the baseless fabric of the vision dissolved. The problem of personal identity is obviated bv the revelation, or reaffirmation, that these characters are figments of a whimsical imagination. And death becomes, therefore, purely an aesthetic necessity, a way of closing, or as Nabokov describes it in one of his later poems, "a question of technique, a neat / enjambment, a melodic fall."[9]

The ending of *Bend Sinister* provides the most outrageous example of the deus ex machina ending in the English novels, when the narrator intervenes to save the protagonist, Adam Krug, from the "logical fate" that has been prepared for him. The events of the novel subject Krug to two different kinds of psychological pressure which become increasingly more intense. In the first place, the government of his country has fallen into the hands of an old schoolmate, Paduk, now a ruthless dictator who demands unthinking fealty and complete submission. He has closed the university at which Krug teaches philosophy and has informed the president that it will remain closed until the entire faculty signs a manifesto supporting the government and abjuring all kinds of dissent. Krug alone refuses to sign, and since he is not only the country's leading thinker but also its only international celebrity, Paduk needs his compliance. He tries to break Krug down by arresting first his close friends and then his acquaintances. Krug holds out, stoutly maintaining his invulnerability and only very slowly making the connection between the disappearance of his friends and his own sneers at the dictator. Paduk eventually recognizes that Krug's only vulnerable spot is his love for his young son David; the boy is seized, and Krug instantly capitulates. The ruler's henchmen bungle their job, however, and David is mistakenly killed. Paduk has now lost his most effective lever for moving Krug, who becomes more obstinate than ever. Paduk offers Krug the lives of twenty-four prisoners (as Satan offers Faustus twenty-four years of life) in exchange for his soul. Krug, unlike Faustus, refuses.

The second kind of pressure actually absorbs more of Krug's thought than do Paduk's machinations. When the novel opens Krug is with his dying wife, Olga, in her hospital room. Olga never regains consciousness, and Krug's grief at her death is complicated by the prospect of having to explain to David what has happened to his mother. His grief gradually abates, but the nagging question of what to say to his eight-year-old son only becomes more insistent. Krug placates David for a while by telling him that Olga was taken on a white hospital train with a white engine to a country by the sea where she is recuperating. But Krug knows this is a temporary expedient: "The picture is pretty, but how long can it stay on the screen? We expect the next slide, but the magic-lantern man has none left" (p. 98). Krug, addressing his thoughts to Olga, acknowledges that it is not really concern for his child's reaction that causes him to hesitate:

Are not these problems so hard to solve because my own mind is not made up yet in regard to your death? My intelligence does not accept the transformation of physical discontinuity into the permanent continuity of a nonphysical element escaping the obvious law, nor can it accept the inanity of accumulating incalculable treasures of thought and sensation, and thought-behind-thought and sensation-behind-sensation, to lose them all at once and forever in a fit of black nausea followed by infinite nothingness. Unquote. [P. 99]

Krug has had to confront death before, when both his parents were killed in an accident. That time he had been able to divert his grief and shock into a chapter of the book he was writing, "wherein he looked straight into the eyesockets of death and called him a dog and an abomination. . . . But could he do it again?" (p. 137). He cannot; nor can he find consolation in a mythology that populates the heavens with the dead in an attempt to remove the terror from "those mirrors of infinite space *qui m'effrayent, Blaise*, as they did you, and where Olga is not" (p. 61), and he dismisses all religions as superstitious, including "that wonderful Jewish sect whose dream of the gentle young rabbi dying on the Roman *crux* had spread over all Northern lands" (p. 193).

These two sources of pressure on Krug's usually calm stolidity finally merge when David is taken away and killed as part of a particularly brutal experiment at the Institute for Abnormal Children. Krug's philosophic rationality has been his main line of defense against both the irrationality of totalitarianism and the irrationality of death. As a philosopher he is particularly adept at what he calls "creative destruction" (p. 173), the ability to debunk popular beliefs by exposing their inherent logical fallacies. In this case, however, his rationality is powerless; death and totalitarianism refuse to be debunked, no matter how fallacious their logic.

It is at this point, with his wife and son dead and Krug himself in prison and threatened with execution, that the narrator, whom Nabokov calls "an anthropomorphic deity impersonated by me" (p. xii), intrudes to save Krug from the awareness that would lead to despair: "It was at that moment, just after Krug had fallen through the bottom of a confused dream and sat up on the straw with a gasp—and just before his reality, his remembered hideous misfortune could pounce on him—it was then that I felt a pang of pity for Adam and slid towards him along an inclined beam of pale light—causing instantaneous madness, but at least saving him from the senseless agony of his logical fate" (p. 233). Nabokov has explained the nature of Krug's madness in the introduction to *Bend Sinister*: Krug, he says, "suddenly perceives the simple reality of things and knows but cannot express in the words of his world that he and his son and his wife and everybody else are merely my whims and megrims" (p. viii).

Krug is then led out into the prison yard to confront Paduk and his lieutenants and the twenty-four prisoners whose lives Paduk has placed in his hands. But Krug is mad, and his madness has at last given him the invulnerability he has claimed all along, but which his very sanity denied him. For Krug this ceremony in which life and death hang in the balance has become a performance, a child's game: "What does it all matter? Ridiculous! Same as those infantile pleasures—Olga and the boy taking part in some silly theatricals, she getting drowned, he losing his life or something in a railway accident. What on earth does it matter?" (p. 236). Krug gleefully rushes at Paduk, exhorting his friends—who have reverted to his childhood companions—to join in the charge. A bullet grazes Krug's ear, and a more deadly one is on the way when both Krug's progress and the bullet's are stopped in mid-sentence:

Just a fraction of an instant before another and better bullet hit him, he shouted again: You, you—and the wall vanished, like a rapidly withdrawn slide, and I stretched myself and got up from among the chaos of written and re-written pages, to investigate the sudden twang that something had made in striking the wire netting of my window. . . . Well, that was all. . . . I knew that the immortality I had conferred on the poor fellow was a slippery sophism, a play upon words. But the very last lap of his life had been happy and it had been proven to him that death was but a question of style. [Pp. 240–41]

The last lap of Krug's life is happy because he relinquishes his fate, and with it his fear, to the dream producer, the author of this particular script. As Ada Veen will explain to Van in a later novel, "In 'real' life we are creatures of chance in an absolute void—unless we be artists ourselves, naturally; but in a good play I feel authored, I feel passed by the board of censors, I feel secure, with only a breathing blackness before me . . . , I feel cuddled in the embrace of puzzled Will . . ., or in that of the much more normal Anton Pavlovich" (Ada, pp. 451–52). Krug's madness and his relief are caused by the revelation that he is authored, cuddled in the embrace of Vladimir Vladimirovich.

The artificial endings of Nabokov's novels, especially of Bend Sinister, work to undercut the reader's propensity to see in these fictions an imitation of "real" life, to empathize with the characters and care about their fates. In his discussion of Gogol's The Government Inspector Nabokov notes that Gogol's readers and audiences have consistently made the mistake of taking his play too literally and failing to recognize that his characters, "whether subject or not to imitation by flesh and blood, were true only in the sense that they were true creatures of Gogol's fancy" (Gogol,

p. 41). He dismisses as a "morbid inclination" the desire to find a "true story" behind every work of fiction, and then speculates about the reasons for this inclination. It may be, he concludes, an instance of that "adoration of the truth which makes little children ask the story-teller 'Did it really happen?' and prevented old Tolstoy in his hyperethical stage from trespassing upon the rights of the deity and creating, as God creates, perfectly imaginary people" (*Gogol*, p. 40). The narrator of *Bend Sinister*, who appears to Adam in a beam of light and in effect introduces himself as Adam's creator, does not share Tolstoy's affliction. His appearance at the end of the novel simply reaffirms what his other intrusions into the narrative have already made clear—that all of the characters are his inventions, and that whatever turns the plot may take are determined by his whim. The egregiousness of this intrusion and its "wantonness," as Frank Kermode has described it,[10] are a means of subverting the plot, disinfecting it of the illusion of reality and, consequently, the illusion of meaning.

The narrator's ploy at the end of this novel is certainly the most outrageous of Nabokov's solution-endings, and the least effective. In a later and better book, *Lolita*, Nabokov raises the same issues, but while the narrator of *Bend Sinister* has to scrap the novel in order to save Krug, *Lolita* gradually shapes its own end, and that end gives to the whole a coherence—and a humaneness—that is missing from *Bend Sinister*. The saving madness that Adam Krug slips into with relief is the same kind of madness that Humbert Humbert flirts with in *Lolita*. Humbert would *like* to believe that he is authored, that his destiny is the climax of a plot, so that he can disclaim moral responsibility for his actions. Similarly, his fatal mistake with Lolita is to believe, at least with half his mind, that she is a work of art, an ideal creature immune to time and change. The endings of *Bend Sinister* and *Lolita* are thematically similar in that both books end with a declaration of the victory of art over death. However, the immortality that the narrator of *Bend Sinister* confers on Krug is, as he admits, only a word-trick. It is not death that art wins its victory over in this case, but a death, a potentiality that never becomes actuality because the artist decides he would prefer it that way. Humbert Humbert ends his narrative by conferring immortality on Lolita, but only after recognizing that neither he nor anyone else can ever confer it on Dolores Haze. The truth that the narrator of *Bend Sinister* permits Krug to see is that an author has absolute power of life and death over his creatures; the truth that Humbert claws his way to is that this fact has very little to do with the way a human life is lived.[11]

Bend Sinister is the most self-reflexive and autocratic of Nabokov's novels, English or Russian. It points to itself as its own authority and incorporates images of its own processes and glosses on its own methods and intentions. The novel offers, in short, a commentary on itself, a kind of reader's guide to *Bend Sinister*. Early in the novel, for example, Nabokov introduces an emblematic image in the little book which Orlik the zoologist opens, only to discover that "it was an empty box with a lone pink peppermint on the bottom" (p. 50). This artificial book, which reappears in Krug's dream, is, like *Bend Sinister*, defined only by its shape, a shape that tricks Orlik into thinking he will find facts or truths—meaning—inside. Parts of a line from Mallarmé, "*sans pitie du sanglot dont j'etais encore ivre*," recur in various combinations throughout the book. While this recurrence itself forms part of the structural patterning of the novel, the meaning of the line provides a self-referential commentary, warning that the pattern may be broken at any time, that endings are in no way beholden to beginnings. The narrator's comment on Krug's dream, which is described as if it were a play, offers a paradigm of the relationship between the narrator and the novel:

But among the producers or stagehands responsible for the setting there has been one . . . it is hard to express it . . . a nameless, mysterious genius who took advantage of the dream to convey his own peculiar code message which has nothing to do with school days or indeed with any aspect of Krug's physical existence, but which links him up somehow with an unfathomable mode of being, perhaps terrible, perhaps blissful, perhaps neither, a kind of transcendental madness which lurks behind the corner of consciousness and which cannot be defined more accurately than this, no matter how Krug strains his brain. [P. 64]

This mysterious genius is of course the narrator-as-anthropomor-phic-deity, and the unfathomable mode of being is the awareness of Krug's own fictiveness.

The long *Hamlet* digression which occurs in the middle of the novel is the most extensive of these self-referential commen-taries, and the section that has given critics of *Bend Sinister* the most trouble. Kermode, for example, has noted that "the func-tion of this digression is extremely complicated." He suggests that it is a civilized way for Krug and his friend Ember to avoid talking about Olga, that it is a "useless but agreeable exercise of intellect," that it is funny, and that Ember's translations of *Hamlet* are "another link with the main theme," which he takes to be the political theme.[12] The function of the digression is compli-cated, but rather than shoring up the political theme of the novel it is actually a parodic rejection of the importance of that theme, a burlesque of the kind of criticism that reduces literature to its plots.

Ember, who has been named literary advisor to the State The-atre under Paduk, is attempting to mount a production of *Ham-let*. He has been instructed to base his production on the extraor-dinary work of the late Professor Hamm, author of "The Real Plot of *Hamlet*." According to Hamm's theory, the real hero of the play is Fortinbras, who steps in to redeem Denmark from the "corruption of civil and military life" (p. 108). The founda-tion of Hamm's theory is his contention that

according to the immemorial rules of the stage what is boded must be embodied: the eruption must come at all cost. In *Ham-let* the exposition grimly promises the audience a play founded upon young Fortinbras' attempt to recover the lands lost by his father to King Hamlet. This is the conflict, this is the plot. To surreptitiously shift the stress from this healthy, vigorous and clearcut Nordic theme to the chameleonic moods of an impo-tent Dane would be, on the modern stage, an insult to deter-minism and common sense. [P. 108]

L. L. Lee has shown that Hamm's theory is made up in part of quotations from various critical comments included in the Furness variorum *Hamlet*.[13] But Hamm also has affinities with the misguided critics of another Nabokov favorite, Gogol.

Hamm's theory, which turns *Hamlet* into a political allegory, is based on a willful misreading of the play, and through it the narrator anticipates and parodies potential misreadings of his novel. The parallels are clear. In the first place, the plot of *Bend Sinister* is a tale of political intrigue, but that plot is as ancillary to the thematic center of the book, located in the chameleonic moods of impotent Krug, as are the political plots of *Hamlet* and *The Government Inspector*. Nabokov has said of Gogol's play that only "simple minds would see in the play a social satire violently volleyed at the idyllic system of official corruption in Russia" (*Gogol*, p. 35). In the second place, much that is boded in *Bend Sinister* is never embodied—most obviously, Krug's death. Several characters appear briefly, or are mentioned, and then never reappear and have no apparent bearing on the course of events in the novel. Two of these characters, Professors Gleeman and Yanovsky, whom the narrator introduces as "newborn homunculi" (p. 38) and then abandons, seem to point directly to all those secondary characters that drift in and out of Gogol's works. In his discussion of *The Government Inspector* Nabokov refers to these characters as "homunculi" and points to their appearance as one of the marks of Gogol's eccentric genius: "The beauty of the thing is that these secondary characters will not appear on the stage later on. . . . A famous playwright has said (probably in a testy reply to a bore wishing to know the secrets of his craft) that if in the first act a shot gun hangs on the wall, it must go off in the last act. But Gogol's guns hang in mid-air and do not go off—in fact the charm of his allusions is exactly that nothing whatever comes of them" (*Gogol*, p. 44). Hamm's *Hamlet* theory parodies the kind of misreading that complex, subtle works of genius invite—especially the works of Nabokov's favorite Olympians, Shakespeare, Gogol, and Nabokov.

Krug and Ember move from Hamm's theory to their own playful discussion of *Hamlet*, which becomes a game of witty, allusive oneupmanship. Krug steers the conversation in this direction to distract Ember, who has suddenly remembered Olga and begun to weep. They talk not of what *Hamlet* means, but of what its words mean and what they suggest, of the etymology of characters' names, of the pictorial possibilities that might be exploited in a film of the play, of colors, shading, nuances of sound and sense. Krug's diversion works; both he and Ember momentarily forget the pressure of too much reality—death and political oppression—by talking of Shakespeare, "a man who had only to breathe on any particle of his stupendous vocabulary to have that particle live and expand and throw out tremulous tentacles until it became a complex image with a pulsing brain and correlated limbs" (p. 119). The word, the image, the pattern: these are what Krug and Ember delight in and what make the autonomous world of *Hamlet* a refuge for them. We can be sure, then, that Krug and Ember would not misread *Bend Sinister*.

George Steiner has suggested that "it would be by no means eccentric to read the major part of Nabokov's opus as a meditation—lyric, ironic, technical, parodistic—on the nature of human language." [14] The novels in which that concern with the nature of language is most obvious are the first three English novels, *The Real Life of Sebastian Knight*, *Bend Sinister*, and *Lolita*. It is understandable that these books would reflect Nabokov's attempts to domesticate his adopted language and synchronize its rhythms with the rhythms of his thought; it is also understandable from this perspective that the last of the three books is the best, the most serenely self-confident, and the most accessible. At the same time, there are tensions in these novels that grow out of another kind of struggle to understand the complex relationship between language and meaning, and it is in *Lolita* that those tensions are most gracefully and convincingly resolved.

Each novel explores the possibilities and limitations of articulate art (Nabokov's useful phrase), and each uses a different mode of art, or genre, as its touchstone. That is, the questions that *Sebastian Knight* raises about language in art are referred to the conventions of the novel; in *Bend Sinister* they are referred to the conventions of the drama, and in *Lolita* to those of poetry. Sebastian Knight is a novelist, and much of what V knows about him he has deduced from Sebastian's novels. V is writing a biography, but the problems he runs into in reconstructing Sebastian's life make him wish that he were a novelist instead. He yearns for "the easy swing of a well-oiled novel" (p. 52) that would give him license to picture "my hero's smooth development from infancy to youth" (p. 20). Such a novel would not have the maddening gaps that V's biography must have. V believes strongly that language and meaning are coextensive, that there is a one-to-one relationship between words and ideas. "No real idea can be said to exist," V says, "without the words made to measure" (p. 84). Consequently, he believes that if he can discover that single word that the dying man in Sebastian's novel discovered, he too will understand all mysteries; if the secret exists, then it must exist in a word. V also believes that setting the right words in the right order—the method of the well-oiled novel—is an avenue to meaning, just as he believes that getting the events of Sebastian's life in the right alignment will lead him to understand the meaning of his life. V is, from Nabokov's perspective, wrong on both counts. At one point in the novel Clare Bishop reminds Sebastian that "a title must convey the color of the book, not its subject" (p. 72). In this book Nabokov suggests that language can convey only the color of thought, and that a novel can be said to mean only insofar as its words approximate the approximations of thought, as a biography, to be accurate, must approximate the amorphousness of a human life. The result is that *Sebastian Knight* is itself an intentionally elusive and ultimately frustrating book.

Bend Sinister makes, on one hand, a greater claim for language than does *Sebastian Knight* by asserting that the artist's words have the power to generate meaning; on the other hand, it undercuts that claim by denying that the meaning generated has any autonomy. The novel is an elegant, intricate house of cards— the "only pure thing" (p. 34) in Krug's study is a copy of Chardin's painting, "House of Cards"—that collapses when the writer stops writing. The narrator of *Bend Sinister* finds metaphors for the method of his book in drama: a play is a self-conscious performance with artificial settings and actors who pretend to be someone else, but only for the duration of the play. When the play is over, its world and its people disappear. The narrator's intrusion at the end of *Bend Sinister*, and the image of his novel as a chaos of written and rewritten pages, is a reminder that whatever meaning the language of *Bend Sinister* has generated is, like Krug's immortality, merely a play upon words.

Humbert Humbert's lament at the beginning of *Lolita*, "I have only words to play with" (p. 34), could just as easily have come from either of the narrators of the other two novels. The difference between Humbert and the others is that Humbert eventually finds his words sufficient. Humbert learns, in fact, that he can capture his nymphet and keep her only in the language of art. His words generate meaning: he did not understand himself or Lolita until he began to write. And they preserve meaning: they immortalize the very thing they have created. The genre that *Lolita* appeals to for its authority is, appropriately, poetry, since the conferring of immortality through art has been one of the most enduring conventions of poetry; the novel begins with echoes of "Annabel Lee" and ends with Humbert thinking of prophetic sonnets. His book is the least claustrophobic and the least arrogant of the three because it is written, as prophetic sonnets are written, for someone else.

Four

Lolita

Lolita is the book which first introduced Nabokov to a wide audience in America (not altogether for the right reasons; it still has not lost its reputation as a "dirty book"). It was also the first of his books to generate much interest among academic critics, and it remains the one which attracts the most attention from them. Not surprisingly, then, among Nabokov's novels *Lolita* has provoked the widest range of readings, and some of the most farfetched. It has been read as a description of the defeat of the dreamer-hero by the corruption of American society; as a book about "the spell exerted by the past"; as a comic treatment of the tensions of family life, with Humbert Humbert in the role of "the parent who sadly suspects that communication has broken down between himself and his child"; as a refutation of the myth of childhood innocence; and as a "mocking exposition of shallow emotionality."[1] Like the hyperbolic pronouncement of John Ray, Jr., *Lolita*'s fictitious editor, that Humbert Humbert's confessions constitute "a tragic tale tending unswervingly to nothing less than a moral apotheosis" (p. 7), these readings of the novel are not so much wrong as they are overingenious. John Ray's mistake is not in finding that the novel has a moral resolution, but in finding the course of the novel "unswerving." Humbert Humbert gropes through his confession, acting as prosecution and defense in his private trial of himself, and in the process touches on as many exploitable themes as one might expect to find in a story as labyrinthine as his. Humbert's narrative is about many things, and its tone varies according to the turns he chooses to take in picking his way through "the maddeningly complex prospect of my past" (p. 15). At the center of that "tangle of thorns" (p. 11), however, is the fixed point of Humbert's obsession with nymphets: *Lolita* is, first and last, the anatomy of an obsession.

Humbert has to go through his experiences twice, blundering through them the first time and then sorting and reordering them as he writes out his narrative, before he can see any meaning in them, any pattern in that tangle of thorns. The narrative he produces is clearly more than a story; it is an attempt at interpretation, clarification, simplification—in short, a commentary on the text of his lived experience. What most distinguishes Humbert's commentary from those produced by Nabokov's other narrators is its consistent confessional quality. Humbert freely admits to the crimes of child rape and murder; he has no reason not to confess these crimes, since the evidence for conviction is all there in the text of the life. The commentary, on the other hand, gives him the chance to establish the radical innocence of his motives. To be convicted Humbert needs only to recall facts; to be pardoned he must ask his audience to *read* his life with the aid of the commentary, to compare it with other written lives, to see that child rape and murder—when we as readers encounter them in a text—can be disturbing but convincing metaphors for a desire for moral and aesthetic perfection.

This desire is, as Humbert believes, innocent enough in itself. When the desire becomes a motive for action, however, Humbert becomes a sociopath, although one who can still convince us of his essential innocence, in part because his desire *is* radical and obsessive. Humbert's aim in his confession becomes clearer when we compare him to the two characters in the novel with whom his affinities are strongest, the moralist John Ray, Jr., and the aesthete Clare Quilty. The chief difference between Ray and Humbert is a matter of degree—the difference between the meliorist and the perfectionist. Ray wishes to defend the publication of Humbert's confession on the grounds that it is useful as a cautionary tale that can remind us readers of the dangers of dropping our moral guard, especially where the rearing of children is concerned. Most of his language is the rhetoric of the unreflecting moralist. For example, Ray defends the erotic passages in Humbert's narrative, those that "a certain type of mind might call 'aphrodisiac,'" on the grounds that they are "strictly functional" in the moral scheme of the book (pp. 6, 7). Humbert makes the same point, but the difference in language is telling; Humbert begs the reader not to skip "these essential pages" that describe his first night as Lolita's lover. "Imagine me; . . . try to discern the doe in me, trembling in the forest of my own iniquity" (p. 131). Ray does, however, admit to some ambivalence; he finds his wonder at the aesthetic appeal of Humbert's prose difficult to reconcile with his obligatory disgust at Humbert's moral lapses: "But how magically his singing violin can conjure up a tendresse, a compassion for Lolita that makes us entranced with the book while abhorring its author!" (p. 7). What Ray does not understand is that Humbert's prose sings in just that way because the prose itself is at once an act of contrition and an acknowledgment that the moral and the aesthetic can merge—not in the text of experience, but in the metaphors of the commentary. Because Ray does not need to accomplish this kind of merger in order to justify himself, he can take note of his own ambivalence and then dismiss it, resisting the appeal of the aesthetic and reverting in the end to the safety of his blandly moralistic stance. Even if we are drawn to the book by its entrancing style, he concludes, our final judgment of its value must be made by moral and ethical standards. Ray can give his final approval to the book because it warns us all of the dangers inherent in childrearing and should encourage us to "apply ourselves with still greater vigilance and vision to the task of bringing up a better generation in a safer world" (p. 8).

While Ray figures in the book only as a very minor character who, as the author of the brief foreword, actually stands outside the arena of the action and is present only as a stylized voice, his importance as an emblematic figure in the psychological scheme of Humbert's narrative is as great as that of his opposite, Clare Quilty. Although Quilty participates in the action of the novel, his actual appearances are few; for most of the book he is only a shadowy presence that first complicates all of Humbert's desires, then focuses all his frustration and rage, and then pricks his conscience. Like Ray, Quilty is an emblematic figure, speaking in the stylized voice of the completely amoral aesthete. The two voices, those of the moralist and the aesthete, do battle for possession of Humbert's own style in the commentary—which, in this book, is the same as saying that they do battle for his soul. If Humbert becomes progressively weakened and ultimately almost paralyzed by his constant, agonized examination of his own motives and his own style, both Ray and Quilty can speak, act, and write with confident assurance precisely because they are unreflecting.

I have called Quilty an amoral aesthete; what Humbert calls him, with more passion and less indirection, is "this semi-automated, subhuman trickster who had sodomized my darling" (p. 297). Quilty succeeds where Humbert fails, as artist and seducer, in large part because he *is*, from Humbert's perspective, a subhuman trickster; that is, because he has no moral scruples and is incapable of love. His complete insensitivity allows him not only to use people for his pleasure, but also to see them as potential raw material for his art. Unlike the more self-conscious Humbert, Quilty can translate the actual person into his own idealized version with no sense of betrayal, no fear of misrepresentation, no anxiety about making his version square with "human reality." He can be seen as a compendium of the impulses of the artist—the Flaubertian, Proustian, Joycean artist—abstracted from the moral being they normally inhabit and given an independent life of their own. For Quilty, therefore, the pursuit of Lolita is only a challenging game, a series of tactical maneuvers across the chessboard of America in an attempt to capture Humbert's queen. Because he is an unfeeling automaton and thus morally and emotionally invulnerable, Quilty can afford to take the risks and play the tricks that make the game more interesting and eventually allow him to win. Similarly, he can write a play for Lolita in which he transforms her into an enchantress and then back into a "down-to-brown-earth lass" (p. 203) without plunging into a nightmare of bewilderment and remorse, because this transformation is, for him, only an artist's neat stylistic device. Humbert attempts a similar kind of transformation of Lolita in the private dramatization of his own desires; he wants desperately to possess the enchantress, to be initiated into her secret mysteries and to find there the end of all desire, but at the same time he is appalled at the damage he must do to the vulnerable child in the process. Quilty, the consummate trickster-artist, does not believe in the reality of his creations or take his games seriously. Humbert the poet manqué suffers the torments of hell because he wants to believe that the patrimonies of poets are real places, that nymphets and enchantresses can be possessed, that fairy children can "play around me forever. Never grow up" (p. 23).

Quilty is an elusive, phantom figure throughout most of the book, using contrived names and appearing in shadowy places. It is this phantom that Humbert hates and determines to kill; he does not even know the identity of his rival until his final interview with Lolita. Although Humbert recognizes that he and Quilty share some characteristics in addition to their sexual preferences—"his genre, his type of humor—at its best at least—the tone of his brain, had affinities with my own" (p. 251)—he never thinks of Quilty as a *doppelgänger* figure; his motives for murder are outrage and a desire for revenge. With Quilty, as with Lolita, Humbert takes his own metaphors too literally; by calling Quilty "subhuman" Humbert performs a mental maneuver that places the killing of such a creature outside the territory in which moral acts are committed. Such a killing would not be murder—just as sexual intercourse with a daemonic nymphet would never be the same as child rape.

The actual killing, however, turns out to be a horrifying nightmare that only increases Humbert's wretchedness: "Far from feeling any relief, a burden even weightier than the one I had hoped to get rid of was with me, upon me, over me. I could not bring myself to touch him to see if he was really dead" (p. 307). He attempts to see this death as a fitting, obligatory end to the farce staged by playwright Quilty, complete with music, dancing, and poetry: Quilty plays the piano, he rises from his chair "like old, gray, mad Nijinski" while Humbert chases him "in a ballet-like stiff bounce" (pp. 304, 305), and Humbert has Quilty read a parody of Eliot's "Ash Wednesday." But Quilty is no longer a mirage, an imaginary villain; he dies a messy, bloody death that startles Humbert into revulsion: "Thomas had something.

It is strange that the tactile sense, which is so infinitely less precious to men than sight, becomes at critical moments our main, if not only, handle to reality. I was all covered with Quilty—with the feel of that tumble before the bleeding" (p. 308). The farcical, movieland destruction of the shape-shifting villain becomes, with a single touch, the nightmare of murder. The expiatory release that Humbert had anticipated may be achieved through the artistic restaging of the murder in the metaphors of the commentary, where Quilty can be appropriately cast as an emblematic figure, but for Humbert the actual killing of the real person is ugly, muddled, untransfigurable.

Humbert had been on the verge of making a similar mistake earlier when he was tempted to kill Charlotte Haze, whom he had courted and married only in order to be near her daughter, Lolita. On an expedition to Hourglass Lake, it occurs to him that he could dispatch his wife easily enough by drowning her in the middle of the lake. He rehearses the drowning mentally and finds it "like some dreadful silent ballet, the male dancer holding the ballerina by her foot and streaking down through watery twilight" (p. 89). This time Humbert is stopped short of actual murder by the obtrusive reality of Charlotte's physical presence: "I could not make myself drown the poor, slippery, big-bodied creature. . . . Were I to catch her by her strong kicking foot; were I to see her amazed look, hear her awful voice; were I still to go through with the ordeal, her ghost would haunt me all my life" (p. 89). Charlotte Haze is spared Quilty's fate because she is, from the beginning, not a mirage but an oppressive, dull, untransfigurable reality.

The ballet imagery that Humbert uses in describing his vision of Charlotte's death by drowning recurs in two other, similar passages—in the description of Quilty's death, which I have cited above, and in Humbert's rhapsodic description of Lolita's tennis game. Watching her play, Humbert feels an "indescribable itch of rapture" (p. 232). He sees her game as in every respect a performance, "the highest point to which I can imagine a young creature bringing the art of make-believe" (p. 233), and he sees Lolita as a willing and skilled performer: "Over and over again she would land an easy one into the net—and merrily mimic dismay by drooping in a ballet attitude, with her forelocks hanging" (p. 235). These "ballet" scenes indicate the pattern of ambivalent responses that make up Humbert's dilemma: the voice of the aesthete urges him to turn the expressions of love and hate into stylized, ritualistic performances that are judged by aesthetic rather than moral standards, and the voice of the moralist—and the tactile feel of flesh—remind him of the price he must pay in guilt and self-loathing.

Another way of approaching Humbert's dilemma is to see him as a character who strains throughout the novel to achieve the reader's perspective—that is, to see *himself* as a character in an elegant fiction. Humbert is in an impossible position (and Nabokov's portrayal of the cruel artist Quilty may include an acknowledgment of his own cruelty in treating Humbert so), since the intensity of his private feelings keeps him painfully aware of his status as a mortal human being, while at the same time he senses that he is the product of a genealogy that is entirely literary. These two irreconcilable senses of the self, as both person and character, are to be found in all of Nabokov's perplexed narrators, but while the others typically struggle to be free of the constricting and frightening feeling that they are characters in someone else's fiction, Humbert struggles in the other direction. He would like to be able to read his life story in the same way we do; if he could, he would rid himself of guilt and moral responsibility, and he would be able to interpret the details of his story, even those that seem most insignificant, as reliable, significant guides to understanding his nature, his behavior, and his fate. Consequently, Humbert looks to his own literary genealogy to find those like-minded precursors whose analogous situations might enlighten or instruct or, more important, justify him. In short, Humbert alludes at every opportunity, and if his allusions serve him badly by only intensifying his confusion, they serve us well by clarifying the psychological conflict that is the source of his confusion.

Humbert's choice of allusions already tells us a lot about his proclivities and about the kind of literary tradition in which he would like to place himself. Appropriately, the writer he appeals to most often is Edgar Allan Poe. Humbert might have said of Poe what he says of Quilty—that "the tone of his brain" had affinities with Humbert's own: Poe, like Humbert, loved a young girl who died prematurely; as a writer, Poe was fascinated by the nature of obsession; and as a theoretician, he insisted that the artist himself must be obsessed with beauty and that the sole aim of art must be aesthetic pleasure, which comes through the evocation of a beauty so perfect it can only be glimpsed and never fully apprehended. At the same time, Poe's characters who share this obsession with the ideal become, because of it, grotesque figures—madmen, murderers, suicides.

Perhaps the strongest affinity between Humbert and Poe, or the strongest indication of their affinity, is found in the kind of language they use when they speak of their own response to the beautiful. Both succeed in conveying a clear sense that, for them, any statement about the nature of the beautiful has both an aesthetic and an erotic import. In Poe's essay on "The Poetic Principle," for example, he includes this explanation of the source of the poet's attraction to the ideal of perfect beauty:

We have still a thirst unquenchable. . . . This thirst belongs to the immortality of Man. It is at once a consequence and an indication of his perennial existence. It is the desire of the moth for the star. It is no mere appreciation of the Beauty before us—but a wild effort to reach the Beauty above. Inspired by an ecstatic prescience of the glories beyond the grave, we struggle, by multiform combinations among the things and thoughts of Time, to attain a portion of that Loveliness whose very elements, perhaps, appertain to eternity alone.[2]

Humbert the enchanted hunter, who several times speaks of himself as a poet, describes his own unquenchable thirst for the perfect bliss of nymphet love in a vocabulary that makes the erotic and the aesthetic indistinguishable. He is dissatisfied with ordinary sex, "that routine rhythm which shakes the world," because he has "caught glimpses of an incomparably more poignant bliss" (p. 20); watching Lolita play tennis produces in him "the teasing delirious feeling of teetering on the very brink of unearthly order and splendor" (p. 232); the real attraction of "pure young forbidden fairy child beauty," Humbert concludes, is that "infinite perfections fill the gap between the little given and the great promised—the great rosegray never-to-be-had" (p. 266).

The allusions to Poe in *Lolita* are numerous and varied. The many references to "Annabel Lee" are obvious enough to require little comment; generally they consist of phrases taken from the poem, sometimes verbatim and sometimes slightly altered. Other Poe allusions, less obvious, have been identified by a number of readers.[3] For example, Humbert, like Poe's William Wilson, kills his "double," then writes out a confession under a pseudonym just before he dies. Both Humbert and Wilson ask for the sympathy of their readers on the grounds that they can see a thread of fatality running through their misdeeds. Clare Quilty's house, Pavor Manor, is reminiscent of Poe's House of Usher, and there are similarities between Humbert's slow stalking of Quilty and Montresor's diabolically methodical murder of Fortunato in "The Cask of Amontillado."

There is one other allusion to a Poe story that has particularly important thematic implications for Humbert's narrative. An allusion to "Ligeia" is incorporated into Humbert's description of his final passionate rendezvous with Annabel Leigh, his first love. The narrator of Poe's story details his consuming love for the beautiful Ligeia, especially his obsession with the mysterious expression of her eyes, the source of which "I was possessed with a passion to discover." Ligeia dies, and the distraught narrator, still haunted by thoughts of her, subsequently marries a woman he does not love. This wife soon falls ill. Her death chamber is a bizarre room lined with "arabesque" tapestries kept constantly in motion by currents of air. As the narrator ministers to his wife he sees, or thinks he sees, drops of a ruby-colored liquid falling from the air into her goblet of wine. The fair-haired Rowena dies, but as the narrator keeps watch by her corpse it stirs into life, then once again subsides into death. The process is repeated several times, the corpse appearing to "struggle with some invisible foe," until finally it arises from the bed and the fallen shroud reveals the dark hair of the reincarnated Ligeia.[4] Humbert and his Annabel, who love each other with a "frenzy of mutual possession" (p. 14), meet in a grove within sight of "the arabesques of lighted windows." Annabel's mouth is "distorted by the acridity of some mysterious potion," and in the heat of their lovemaking she "would draw away with a nervous toss of her hair, and then come darkly near." Humbert and Annabel are interrupted before their passion is consummated, and for Humbert "the ache remained with me, and that little girl with her seaside limbs and ardent tongue haunted me ever since—until at last, twenty-four years later, I broke her spell by incarnating her in another" (p. 16–17).

This description, which comes early in the book and freely mixes the "Annabel Lee" and "Ligeia" allusions, sets the problem that Humbert seeks to understand and finally to resolve in the rest of his narrative. It is the same problem that Poe sets— but does not resolve—for the characters in many of his poems and stories and for the hypothetical poet in "The Poetic Principle." (It is interesting to note that Humbert and Annabel are interrupted by a character who has no other role in the novel, a family friend of the Leighs named Dr. Cooper, who "ponderously limped into the garden" to fetch Annabel away [p. 17]. His appearance suggests that Nabokov intended to notify his readers that in *Lolita* he was returning to some matters that were left unresolved when James Fenimore Cooper limped into the American romanticist's garden, with his sturdy democratic beau ideal in tow.) Humbert, haunted by the memory of a perfect bliss glimpsed but never possessed, spends the rest of his life in a mad, frenzied search for the perfect incarnation of an ideal which, he now believes, was once tantalizingly near. He acknowledges that his obsession with nymphets is a kind of madness, but insists that its source is an excess of aesthetic sensitivity: "The gentle and dreamy regions through which I crept were the patrimonies of poets—*not* crime's prowling ground" (p. 133).

Humbert also calls to his defense two other poets, in addition to Poe, who loved young girls—Dante and Petrarch. Granting himself a place in this time-honored tradition, however, is not sufficient to save him from the "atrocious, unbelievable, unbearable, and, I suspect, eternal horror" that gradually overwhelms him (p. 171). Early in his narrative Humbert indicates, without elaborating, the reason for the horror: "And what is most singular is that she . . . has individualized the writer's ancient lust, so that above and over everything else there is—Lolita" (pp. 46–47). The source of Humbert's despair is his inability to recognize that the kingdom by the sea which is the true home of his nymphets is a country of the mind, and that sanity, morality, and even love require a clear distinction between the ideal and the actual, between art and life. His lust for the poet's ideal is transferred onto an unremarkable, not particularly lovable child, and eventually becomes for him an expense of spirit in a waste of shame. His horror is the result of moral revulsion at the knowledge that in his pursuit of an irrational ideal he has deprived Lolita of the right to her childhood.

While the references to Poe are the clearest and most obvious allusions in the book (Nabokov's working title for *Lolita* was *A Kingdom by the Sea*), they actually form part of a network of interrelated allusions to a group of writers whose themes and preoccupations Humbert would find particularly congenial— among them Keats and Proust. The obsessive, driven nature of Humbert's love and the solipsistic quality of its pleasures, which make it strike both Humbert and the reader as at once heroic and diseased, recall the very similar treatment of love in Proust's *Remembrance of Things Past*. The sense that Humbert's rendering of the psychological texture of love in *Lolita* is deliberately Proustian is reinforced by an apt allusion early in the book. Humbert records that as a student he once wrote a paper on "The Proustian theme in a letter from Keats to Benjamin Bailey" (p. 18). The letter referred to is surely the one of November 22, 1817, in which Keats discusses an idea which is indeed Proustian, but also close to Poe's description of the sources of aesthetic pleasure: "Have you never by being surprised with an old Melody— in a delicious place—by a delicious voice, felt over again your very speculations and surmises at the time it first operated on your soul—do you not remember forming to yourself the singer's face more beautiful [than] it was possible and yet with the elevation of the Moment you did not think so—even then you were mounted on the Wings of Imagination so high—that the Prototype must be here after."[5]

A melody from the haunting Vinteuil sonata, with its complex associations with sensory memory and the timelessness of art, becomes one of the leitmotifs of Proust's novel. In the final volume, *The Past Recaptured*, Marcel discusses Swann's misinterpretation of the mysterious appeal of the sonata: "Was this perhaps that happiness which the little phrase of the sonata promised to Swann and which he, because he was unable to find it in artistic creation, mistakenly assimilated to the pleasures of love, was this the happiness of which long ago I was given a presentiment—as something more supraterrestrial even than the mood evoked by the little phrase of the sonata?"[6] Both Swann and Humbert are defeated by the sheer force of their own desires, which originate in the vague presentiment that life ought to offer more than it does, that if approximations of happiness are possible then complete happiness should also be possible, that the aesthetic pleasures art sometimes affords us must surely have a satisfying counterpart in erotic love.

In the passages I have quoted from Proust, Keats, and Poe ("The Poetic Principle"), these three thoroughly dissimilar writers all suggest that the ultimate source of aesthetic desire and aesthetic pleasure is located outside the boundaries of mortal experience. The presence of the three writers in *Lolita* helps to clarify a statement Nabokov makes in the afterword to the novel that has been frequently cited as a kind of distillation of Nabokov's aesthetic credo: "For me a work of fiction exists only insofar as it affords me what I shall bluntly call aesthetic bliss, that is a sense of being somehow, somewhere, connected with other states of being where art (curiosity, tenderness, kindness, ecstasy) is the norm" (pp. 316–17). Nabokov's statement makes much more sense when we see it in the context of the other passages I have cited, and as a comment on that particular strain of the romantic tradition in literature, a strain that is inherently religious, of which both Humbert and Nabokov are inheritors. However, the passage (especially the parenthetical part) becomes most clear when we compare it to yet another passage in Proust which—given the similarity of diction and syntax—may well have been a source of Nabokov's statement. Proust's passage appears in *The Captive*, in Marcel's description of the death of the writer Bergotte, who collapsed while standing in front of Vermeer's *Street in Delft*, admiring the scrupulous care with which Vermeer had rendered a small patch of yellow wall. After describing Bergotte's sudden death, Marcel goes on to question whether Bergotte is "permanently dead," or whether the impulse which prompts a talented artist like Bergotte or Vermeer to strain for perfection in his work is not in fact an indication that there are worlds beyond this one; such impulses may, Marcel speculates, actually be "obligations contracted in a former life": "All these obligations which have not their sanction in our present life seem to belong to a different world, founded upon kindness, scrupulosity, self-sacrifice, a world entirely different from this."[7] Perhaps the most interesting and important similarity between Nabokov's statement and Proust's is that in the other "world" which both imagine, there is no distinction made—as there is in this world—between the response to beauty (or "aesthetic bliss") and the desire to be kind, tender, and self-sacrificing.[8]

While the treatments of love and desire in *Lolita* and *Remembrance of Things Past* are similar, especially in their tonality, the strategies and intentions of the two books are clearly different. One of the most obvious differences is that Humbert is finally able to break out of the prison of solipsistic obsession by recognizing that in this life "aesthetic bliss" and erotic love are entirely different things. Unlike Proust's Swann, Humbert lives long enough (although just long enough) to resolve the conflict between moral revulsion and aesthetic desire, the beastly and the beautiful, that has characterized his entire affair with Lolita. Whereas Swann needed to break the habit of seeing his Odette every day in order to be able to fall out of love with her, Humbert's forced separation from his Lolita frees him from obsession with the nymphet and so allows him to acknowledge the much simpler, though much more painful, emotion of normal love for another human being.

Humbert rediscovers Lolita, after having lost her for three years, in a clapboard shack at the end of a dirt road. The suntanned fairy child is now pale, worn, hugely pregnant Dolly Schiller. In one of the most moving and convincing passages in the book Humbert announces his relinquishment of the nymphet and his recovery of the mortal, changeable woman:

I looked and looked at her, and knew as clearly as I know I am to die, that I loved her more than anything I had ever seen or imagined on earth, or hoped for anywhere else. She was only the faint violet whiff and dead leaf echo of the nymphet I had

rolled myself upon with such cries in the past; an echo on the
brink of a russet ravine, with a far wood under a white sky,
and brown leaves choking the brook, and one last cricket in the
crisp weeds . . . but thank God it was not that echo alone that I
worshiped. . . . I insist the world know how much I loved my
Lolita, *this* Lolita, pale and polluted, and big with another's
child, but still gray-eyed, still sooty-lashed, still auburn and al-
mond, still Carmencita, still mine. . . . No matter, even if those
eyes of hers would fade to myopic fish, and her nipples swell
and crack, and her lovely young velvety delicate delta be
tainted and torn—even then I would go mad with tenderness
at the mere sight of your dear wan face, at the mere sound of
your raucous young voice, my Lolita. [Pp. 279–80]

One measure of the immense psychological distance Humbert
has traveled is indicated by comparing this lyrical description of
the russet ravine and crisp weeds of his mental landscape with
his earlier description of the actual approach to Lolita's house:

Hunter Road was miles away, in an even more dismal district,
all dump and ditch, and wormy vegetable garden, and shack,
and gray drizzle, and red mud, and several smoking stacks
in the distance. I stopped at the last "house"—a clapboard
shack with two or three similar ones farther away from the
road and a waste of withered weeds all around. [P. 271]

Surely the clearest indication that Humbert has freed himself
from his self-destructive obsession is that he can now, gratefully,
acknowledge his own mortality as well as the physical evidence
of aging in the mortal Lolita, even though she has begun to give
obvious signs of becoming only a slightly altered version of her
mother—the woman Humbert despised for being fleshy, vapid,
and unforgivably ordinary. To love the real woman makes it possible to give up the hopeless attempt to possess the nymphet,
but to retain the image of the nymphet under an impossible
white sky makes tolerable the demotic landscape—hopeless in
its own way—of dumps and mud and smokestacks.
    The story of Humbert's experiences ends with the end of two
lives—the killing of Quilty and the destruction of Dolores Haze's

childhood. Throughout most of his narrative Humbert struggles with the guilt he feels for the second of these murders; he feels no remorse for the first: "Had I come before myself, I would have given Humbert at least thirty-five years for rape, and dismissed the rest of the charges" (p. 310). His various allusions in the course of the commentary on his experiences are one part of his defense against the charges he brings against himself. By seeing himself in a purely literary context Humbert attempts to shed the burden of moral responsibility for his crimes. He constantly insists that there is a fatality to his story: things have been arranged in advance for him by a personified "McFate"; he struggles futilely to "break some pattern of fate in which I obscurely felt myself being enmeshed" (p. 217), only to discover that he had misinterpreted "the designations of doom" (p. 219). In the process of writing his own book around himself, however, Humbert has finally come to the realization that neither he nor the real Lolita was a poet's invention: he was a free moral agent who took advantage of a vulnerable and dependent child. John Ray, Jr., is thus not too far off the mark when he says that Lolita ends with a moral apotheosis; the novel certainly has a moral resolution, and part of its meaning and force comes through Humbert's gradual acclimation to the perplexing landscape of his new country and his implicit acknowledgment that the literary sources he has looked to for justification are demonstrably poor guides to the vagaries of life in contemporary middle-class America.[9]

Humbert pursues his erotic fantasies across a landscape that is at once a constant source of amazement to him and a perfect complement to his obsession. Early in his account he explains that "What drives me insane is the twofold nature of this nymphet— of every nymphet, perhaps; this mixture in my Lolita of tender dreamy childishness and a kind of eerie vulgarity, stemming from the snub-nosed cuteness of ads and magazine pictures" (p. 46). If the moralist in Humbert is shocked by this duality in so young a child, the displaced European in him is equally shocked by the twofold nature of young America, which reflects exactly the same disturbing combination of innocence and vulgarity that Humbert finds in his nymphets. The American wilds are "beautiful, heart-rendingly beautiful, those wilds, with a quality of

wide-eyed, unsung, innocent surrender" (p. 170), but the American landscape also spawns its vulgar Kumfy Kabins, whose
walls Humbert suspects of hiding unimaginable "twists of lust"
(p. 118), its billboards and gas stations, and its tourist towns
flaunting their curiosity shops and phony colonial architecture.
    The several allusions in *Lolita* to T. S. Eliot's "Gerontion" take
on a special significance in the context of Humbert's bewildered
response to the American setting. The most important of these
occurs in the description of Humbert's initial meeting with Rita,
the woman he credits with saving him from the madhouse after
Lolita's escape: "I picked her up one depraved May evening
somewhere between Montreal and New York, or more narrowly,
between Toylestown and Blake, at a darkishly burning bar under the sign of the Tigermoth, where she was amiably drunk"
(p. 260). The conjunction of "Blake" and "Tigermoth" points to
Blake's poem "The Tiger," and so, appropriately, to Blake's treatment of the opposition of innocence and experience. The "Gerontion" allusions continue the same theme, although somewhat
more coyly. In addition to the backward "t s elyot" hidden in
"Toylestown," Nabokov's sentence contains what seem to be arbitrary echoes of this passage from Eliot's poem:

> Signs are taken for wonders. "We would see a sign!"
> The word within a word, unable to speak a word,
> Swaddled with darkness. In the juvenescence of the year
> Came Christ the tiger
>
> In depraved May, dogwood and chestnut, flowering judas,
> To be eaten, to be divided, to be drunk.

The primary function of this allusion becomes clear if we go beyond Eliot's poem to the source on which he drew for part of the
imagery of the passage—Henry Adams's description of spring
in the American South:

> Here and there a negro cabin alone disturbed the dogwood
> and the judas-tree, the azalea and the laurel. The tulip and the
> chestnut gave no sense of struggle against a stingy nature.
> The soft, full outlines of the landscape carried no hidden hor-

rors of glaciers in its bosom. The brooding heat of the profligate vegetation; the cool charm of the running water; the terrific splendor of the June thundergust in the deep and solitary woods, were all sensual, animal, elemental. No European spring had shown him the same intermixture of delicate grace and passionate depravity that marked the Maryland May.[10]

The same combination of grace and depravity that Adams finds perplexing and alien in the southern landscape is exactly the phenomenon that Humbert finds so disconcerting about America *and* about his nymphets.[11]

Lolita the ideal consumer, with her "combination of naïveté and deception, of charm and vulgarity" (pp. 149–50), is, at least from the perspective of an outsider like Humbert, a personification of the exasperating American phenomenon. She is ingenuousness and innocence despoiled by a penchant for tawdriness and a taste for the sham. Humbert, in his agonies of self-reproach for what he has done to a helpless child, at times takes on himself the responsibility for the despoliation of an entire, helpless country: "And I catch myself thinking today that our long journey had only defiled with a sinuous trail of slime the lovely, trustful, dreamy, enormous country that by then, in retrospect, was no more to us than a collection of dog-eared maps, ruined tour books, old tires, and her sobs in the night—every night, every night—the moment I feigned sleep" (p. 178).

Some of the Americans in the novel are as naive about Europeans as Humbert is about America and Americans. For example, while Humbert sees himself as a depraved debaucher, the product of "sweet, mellow, rotting Europe" (p. 283), Charlotte Haze assumes that since he is European he must be reserved and even a little prim: " 'Your old-world reticence, your sense of decorum may be shocked by the boldness of an American girl!' " (p. 70). If Humbert tends to think of himself as the jaded European corrupter of American innocence, his narrative actually parodies the oversimplicity of such an idea. From the reader's point of view the most corrupt character in the novel is certainly Clare Quilty, who was born in New Jersey, and it is Lolita the American innocent who volunteers to show astonished Humbert what sexual intercourse is all about. The corruption of America, as Nabokov defines it in *Lolita*, is too tawdry to be tragic, and in fact, that corruption itself is finally a matter of point of view. Charlotte Haze, in speaking of Lolita, summarizes the two irreconcilable attitudes toward America—the insider's and the outsider's—that are set against each other in *Lolita*: "You see," Charlotte says, "*she* sees herself as a starlet; *I* see her as a sturdy, healthy, but decidedly homely kid. This, I guess, is at the root of our troubles" (p. 67). The diversion of romantic idealism into the pursuit of cheapness, cuteness, and bad taste isn't distressing to the Americans; only Humbert the outsider is shocked by what he sees, as he is shocked to find that his Lolita is not so innocent as he thought and that America is not virginal, not edenic, and "never Arcadian" (p. 170).

The particular themes I have been discussing—the corruption of an innocent romantic vision, the juxtaposition of an alluring, impossible ideal and a circumscribing, tawdry reality—suggest a comparison between *Lolita* and *Madame Bovary*.[12] Nabokov encourages the comparison by explicit allusions to Flaubert in the novel: "We came to know—*nous connûmes*, to use a Flaubertian intonation" (p. 147), Humbert writes, and Lolita arranges her first trysts with Quilty by pretending to be taking piano lessons from "a Miss Emperor (as we French scholars may conveniently call her)" (p. 204)—an allusion to the Mlle. Lempereur from whom Emma Bovary pretended to be taking her piano lessons. Humbert also notices that Quilty looks a lot like his cousin Gustave, and if this is another allusion to Gustave Flaubert, then it is the most interesting of all. Quilty is like Flaubert in his clinically detached, consistently unemotional manipulation of Lolita, the heroine of this novel. The obvious difference, of course, is that Quilty's attitude toward Lolita can be judged by moral and ethical standards, since those are the ones we apply to the relationships among characters, while Flaubert's pitiless dissection of Emma Bovary is a stylistic strategy that has little to do with morality or ethics. Consequently, we are likely to abhor Quilty as a character for exactly the same reasons that we admire Flaubert as a writer. Our responses to Humbert and our demands on him, on the other hand, are more complicated, since he is both the lover of the heroine, like Quilty, and the author of her book, like Flaubert. As a character, he must release Lolita and destroy

Quilty, thus restoring the moral balance among the characters, before we grant him the privilege of authorial disinterestedness in writing about them.

The most important differences between Nabokov's novel and Flaubert's are clearest in the endings, in the summary pronouncements that Humbert and Charles Bovary make on all that has gone before, and in the action Humbert chooses to take and the inaction Bovary chooses. In his last interview with Emma's lover Rodolphe, Charles Bovary absolves himself, Rodolphe, and everyone else of the responsibility for Emma's suicide and his own defeat. "I can't blame you for it," he tells Rodolphe; "Fate willed it this way."[13] Humbert, who is clearly aware of the similarity of his tale of frustrated desire to Flaubert's, is tempted to adopt Bovary's resignation and throw the responsibility for his predicament onto McFate, the disinterested pursuer. But Humbert eventually settles on a much different and, appropriately, much more American kind of resolution. He chooses to grant himself both the right to revenge and the right to hold himself and others morally responsible for their actions. When Quilty steals Lolita away on the Fourth of July, Humbert, although unaware at the time of the significance of the day, consoles himself by thinking of his own independence: "To myself I whispered that I still had my gun, and was still a free man—free to trace the fugitive, free to destroy my brother" (p. 249). Humbert stalks Quilty, summons him before an impromptu bar of justice, wrestles with him in a scene that he says should remind older readers of "the obligatory scene in the Westerns of their childhood" (p. 301), then carries out the sentence of death he imposed on Quilty for the crime of taking advantage of a sinner's essential innocence. Once the villain is dispatched, Humbert then turns to his own moral accounting, freely accepting the responsibility for having "disregarded all laws of humanity" (p. 308) and for having denied Dolores Haze a part in the "concord" (p. 310) of voices coming from ordinary children at play.

As a child, Humbert says, he envisioned the Appalachian region of America as "a gigantic Switzerland or even Tibet, all mountain, glorious diamond peak upon peak, giant conifers, *le montagnard émigré* in his bear skin glory, and *Felis tigris goldsmithi*, and Red Indians under the catalpas. That it all boiled down to a measly suburban lawn and a smoking garbage incinerator, was appalling" (p. 212). Humbert has learned the hard way that his romantic, Chateaubriandesque vision of America belongs, like his vision of Lolita as the perfect nymphet, only to imagination and art.[14] The real America, like the real Dolores, is disappointingly flawed but still endearing in its naïveté and its incredible, persistent belief in the possibility of justice and the happy, self-sufficient life. Humbert thus concludes his book with two farewells. The first is addressed to the very American Mrs. Richard Schiller, who has enthusiastically and optimistically set off with her new husband for Alaska, the last American frontier. To her he extends a touchingly paternal, genuinely loving wish for a long and happy life. The second is addressed to the imaginary Lolita, the innocent, pure, aesthetically thrilling nymphet who is the invention of his own energetic imagination. That Lolita Humbert the poet is now free to celebrate and immortalize: "I am thinking of aurochs and angels, the secret of durable pigments, prophetic sonnets, the refuge of art. And this is the only immortality you and I may share, my Lolita" (p. 311). That Lolita belongs with other enchanting, remote, and impossible beings. She is a creature of Humbert's imagination, and the only life she will have is the imagined, immortal one Humbert has conferred on her through his art.

Five

Pnin

Timofey Pnin, annotator par excellence, might have had a field day with the novel *Pnin* had he taken any interest at all in contemporary fiction. A meticulous scholar who delights in details, Pnin can straighten out the chronology of *Anna Karenina* for an acquaintance who is reading the book for the seventh time, and pinpoint for him the inconsistencies in it; he knows the birth and death dates of his favorite writers; he can give an ex tempore dissertation on the confusion between *vair* and *verre* in the evolution of the Cinderella story; he can document the first mention of various sports in literature; as a researcher, one of his greatest pleasures is finding and correcting errors in the documentation of others. Pnin, in short, cannot abide imprecision and inconsistency. "It was the world that was absent-minded," the narrator observes, "and it was Pnin whose business it was to set it straight" (p. 13).

Surely, then, Pnin would have had something to say about the carelessness with which the narrator of *Pnin* handles details. For example, the narrator mentions that in the spring of 1911 Pnin was thirteen years old and he, the narrator, was twelve; yet five years later in the summer of 1916 he was only sixteen, while Pnin was properly eighteen. In addition, he first gives 1925 as the year Pnin met his wife, Liza, yet later he speaks of that meeting as occurring "in the early twenties" (p. 179). He cannot be any more specific about the beginning of his acquaintance with Pnin's

good friend Chateau than to place it in the summer of 1935 or
1936. Pnin would certainly have footnoted and cross-referenced
some other oddities in the narrator's account, such as the appearance of that ubiquitous couple, Christopher and Louise
Starr of the fine arts department, who turn up later as the psy-
chologists Louis and Christine Stern, then as the analyst's dolls
Lou and Tina, and finally as Chris and Lew, "a pair of twittering
young Englishmen" (p. 180). Or the appearance of two apparently unrelated minor characters with the same name, the American Bob Horn and the Russian Robert Karlovich Horn.

Pnin might very well have been able to sort out these matters
for us, or perhaps to explain them as gracefully as he explained
Tolstoy's inconsistent chronology as an instance of the difference
between Lyovin's spiritual time and Vronsky's physical time,
"the best example of relativity in literature that is known to me"
(p. 130). For our part as readers, these matters are troublesome
enough, but less troublesome than the more difficult problem of
how to suspend disbelief and accept the veracity of the narrator's very intimate portrait of a man with whom he has only a
slight acquaintance. The problem is compounded because we
would like very much to believe in the reality of this gentle, vulnerable, unself-conscious Pnin, who feels sorry for thirsty squir-
rels and hungry dogs, frequents a failing restaurant purely out
of sympathy, despises gossip and intrigue, and is capable of
completely selfless, lifelong devotion to the things he loves. Yet
we resist putting full faith in the account of this character because the narrator keeps intruding to remind us that it is *his* account and thus, indirectly, that Pnin—at least Pnin in his private
moments, and there are many in the book—is his invention. We
would prefer an invisible narrator to whom we could willingly
grant the privilege of omniscience, who would allow us to main-
tain our aesthetic double standard and acknowledge the fictiveness of *Pnin* but not of Timofey Pnin, to delight in the real toad
we find in the imaginary garden. The narrator seems almost to
warn us not to take his story too seriously, or at least not too
literally. He confesses that his recollections of the few encounters he has had with Pnin are hazy and that he and Pnin disagree on some of the details of those encounters; Pnin even
accuses him in public of being a "dreadful inventor" (p. 185).

Two of his sources of information about Pnin are clearly unreliable—Eric Wind, the psychiatrist for whom Liza left Pnin, and Jack Cockerell, who sees Pnin as a buffoon, the campus character who lends himself well to comic imitation.

The narrator also drops enough clues for the alert reader to recognize that he played a major part in the events that led to Pnin's ill-fated marriage to Liza. He and Liza had a brief affair in Paris that left the narrator unmoved and Liza so moved that she attempted suicide when the affair ended. She married Pnin, on the advice of her analyst friends and after warning the narrator that she would marry someone else if he didn't come through with a proposal immediately, as therapy for her depression. Liza is vain, shallow, histrionic, and flighty—and Pnin loves her devotedly. She leaves Pnin for Eric Wind, a man who "understood her 'organic ego'" (p. 46), returns to Pnin briefly on two occasions when she needs his help, leaves Wind for an American named Church, then leaves him for an Italian art dealer. The narrator is thus indirectly responsible for a large part of Pnin's sadness and sense of loss. When the narrator notes on one occasion that a remark Pnin happened to hear but paid little attention to "now bothered and oppressed him, as does, in retrospection, a blunder we have made, a piece of rudeness we have allowed ourselves, or a threat we have chosen to ignore" (pp. 79–80), the reader begins to suspect that the narrator's motives for writing about Pnin are not disinterested, that he may be trying to rid himself of a lingering regret that now bothers and oppresses him. He protests, almost too much, that Pnin is his friend; he points out that the letter to the editor of the *New York Times* that Pnin proudly carries in his wallet was written with his help, and that the lady at the American consulate in Paris who helped facilitate Pnin and Liza's departure for America was a relative of his. The narrator's account of Pnin is, it appears, a demonstration of the "amazing fact" that V in *The Real Life of Sebastian Knight* found so hard to understand, "that a man writing of things which he really felt at the time of writing, could have had the power to create simultaneously—and out of the very things which distressed his mind—a fictitious and faintly absurd character" (*Knight*, p. 114).

The unusual narrative strategy of *Pnin* eventually lures the reader into a characteristically Nabokovian trap by refusing to conform to his expectations and jostling his preconceptions at every turn: what in the world are we to do with the paradox of an unreliable first-person omniscient narrator? This elaborate, carefully laid trap—baited with the most appealing character in Nabokov's novels—in the end offers the reader an object lesson in the nature of the Nabokovian art of fiction. The first and most elementary precept of that lesson is that a character who distorts some details and invents others is no more unreliable than the author who created the character and the details in the first place. The narrator of the story of Pnin is in fact imitating the creator of *Pnin*, a man he strongly resembles. Both are Anglo-Russian writers who emigrated to America, both were born in Saint Petersburg in the spring of 1899, both are named Vladimir Vladimirovich, and both are amateur lepidopterists. These similarities do not lead us to conclude, as some readers have done, that the narrator *is* Vladimir Nabokov. Rather, they serve to nudge us into the recognition that both are "dreadful inventors" whose fictions, rooted and grounded though they are in the real, take whatever liberties with the real these inventors may choose, in order to make of it an aesthetic whole that satisfies their own whims. Each of them is, as Nabokov has said of another, hypothetical artist, a "forger . . . constructing a mosaic out of genuine odds and ends with his own mortar."[1]

The clearest example of the narrator's capricious imagination at work occurs in what is, significantly, the most sentimentally weighted scene in the book. This scene culminates a series of events that have conspired first to give Pnin the greatest happiness and emotional security he has had since coming to America, and then to snatch them away again. Pnin is content with his job at Waindell College and delighted with the progress of his research, and he has finally, after years of being a nomad, found the house of his dreams. He invites his friends to a "house-heating" party to celebrate his good fortune; the party also gives him a chance to display the splendid new punch bowl he has received as a gift from Liza's son, Victor. The marvelous bowl was "one of those gifts whose first impact produces in the recipient's mind a colored image, a blazoned blur, reflecting with such emblematic force the sweet nature of the donor that the tangible attributes of the thing are dissolved, as it were, in this pure inner blaze, but suddenly and forever leap into brilliant being when praised by an outsider to whom the true glory of the object is unknown" (p. 153).

After the party, the success of which provides the capstone to Pnin's happiness, Pnin's friend and ally Professor Hagen remains behind with an unenviable task to perform: he must tell Pnin that he is going to be fired from Waindell and thus will lose not only his job but his beloved house as well. Hagen delivers the cruel message and departs, leaving Pnin alone with his shocked disappointment, a stack of dirty dishes, and the new bowl:

> He prepared a bubble bath in the sink for the crockery, glass, and silverware, and with infinite care lowered the aquamarine bowl into the tepid foam. Its resonant flint glass emitted a sound full of muffled mellowness as it settled down to soak. . . . He groped under the bubbles, around the goblets, and under the melodious bowl, for any piece of forgotten silver—and retrieved a nutcracker. Fastidious Pnin rinsed it, and was wiping it, when the leggy thing somehow slipped out of the towel and fell like a man from a roof. He almost caught it—his fingertips actually came into contact with it in mid-air, but this only helped to propel it into the treasure-concealing foam of the sink, where an excruciating crack of broken glass followed upon the plunge.
>
> Pnin hurled the towel into a corner and, turning away, stood for a moment staring at the blackness beyond the threshold of the open back door. A quiet, lacy-winged little green insect circled in the glare of a strong naked lamp above Pnin's glossy bald head. He looked very old, with his toothless mouth half open and a film of tears dimming his blank, unblinking eyes. Then, with a moan of anguished anticipation, he went back to the sink and, bracing himself, dipped his hand deep into the foam. A jagger of glass stung him. Gently he removed a broken goblet. The beautiful bowl was intact. He took a fresh dish towel and went on with his household work. [Pp. 171–73]

The narrator lingers over this intense moment, exposing defenseless, pitiful Pnin to the strong glare of his narrative, and toying with both the reader's emotions and Pnin's in the terrible interval between the crack of broken glass and the discovery that the bowl was safe. (Pnin is caught in this passage from the very perspective that Eliot's Prufrock feared so, exposing to prying eyes his baldness and his vulnerability.) It is as if the narrator also pauses during that interval, lifting his pen while he decides the fate of his helpless character. Having chosen to leave Pnin and his bowl intact, the narrator can then return, like Pnin, to the business at hand: he can take a fresh sheet of paper, begin a new chapter, and go on with his work.

This scene in which Pnin is saved from complete despair is similar in its effect to the closing scene in *Bend Sinister*, in which Adam Krug is saved from too much awareness: in both cases we are permitted to see the narrator-as-anthropomorphic-deity at work, creating the private world of a character for whom, at times, he feels pity. In that world fate is much kinder and more sympathetic to the emotional needs of the character and the reader than it is in the "real" world, because it is determined by the forces of imagination, which, Nabokov once said, "in the long run are the forces of good" (*The Eye*, p. iv). The kindness of the narrators in *Pnin* and *Bend Sinister* is arbitrarily bestowed, in defiance of both logic and the tendencies of their own narratives. But in both cases the manipulating narrator offers a justification for his choice of emotional consonance over logic by contrasting his arbitrary kindness with the wanton cruelty that the other deity permits in *his* created world—cruelty that is represented in both books by the slaughtering of innocents that goes on under totalitarian governments.[2] Pnin's first sweetheart, Mira Belochkin, died in a German concentration camp, and the painful knowledge of her fate has since threatened to undermine Pnin's sanity:

In order to exist rationally, Pnin had taught himself, during the last ten years, never to remember Mira Belochkin—not because, in itself, the evocation of a youthful love affair, banal and brief, threatened his peace of mind (alas, recollections of his marriage to Liza were imperious enough to crowd out any former romance), but because, if one were quite sincere with oneself, no conscience, and hence no consciousness, could be expected to subsist in a world where such things as Mira's death were possible. One had to forget—because one could not live with the thought that this graceful, fragile, tender young woman with those eyes, that smile, those gardens and snows in the background, had been brought in a cattle car to an extermination camp and killed by an injection of phenol into the heart, into the gentle heart one had heard beating under one's lips in the dusk of the past. . . . She was selected to die and was cremated only a few days after her arrival in Buchenwald, in the beautifully wooded Grosser Ettersberg, as the region is resoundingly called. It is an hour's stroll from Weimar, where walked Goethe, Herder, Schiller, Wieland, the inimitable Kotzebue and others. [Pp. 134–35]

In his descriptions of Pnin's private moments, such as the dish-washing scene, the narrator is providing his invented character with an alternative world in which beautiful, adored things do not have to be destroyed. The proximity of the poets' Weimar to Buchenwald is a reminder that, while the very real horrors of Buchenwald cannot be denied, there can and do exist what Nabokov once described as "other states of being where art (curiosity, tenderness, kindness, ecstasy) is the norm."[3]

Nabokov's self-conscious, involuted novels frequently contain analogues of their own themes and methods—which in an art so insistent on its artifice become almost indistinguishable. *Pnin* provides an analogue of its method in Pnin's pet project, the "great work on Old Russia, a wonderful dream mixture of folklore, poetry, social history, and *petite histoire*" (p. 39), in which "a choice of Russian Curiosities, Customs, Literary Anecdotes, and so forth would be presented in such a way as to reflect in miniature *la Grande Histoire*—Major Concatenations of Events" (p. 76). Pnin's opus is to be a commentary, a sustained footnote that fleshes out the skeleton of historical fact and gives it life. The narrator also begins with the bare bones of personal history— major concatenations of events in the life of Timofey Pnin, himself a Russian Curiosity—and then supplies his own commentary, a dream mixture of fact and fiction. As frequently happens with Nabokov's commentators (including Pnin himself), however, eventually "the quest overrides the goal, and a new organism is formed, the parasite so to speak of the ripening fruit"

(p. 143). For Pnin the parasite is the intellectual pleasure of re-search, while for the narrator it is the psychological pleasure of creating an aesthetically and emotionally satisfying mosaic out of genuine odds and ends.

Pnin is studded with reminders that in the special world of Nabokov's fiction truth is compounded of the actual and the imaginary, and that the desire to distinguish between the two is an impulse that is sometimes best left outside the door. Within that world life imitates art as often as art imitates life. For exam-ple, the two "identically framed" pictures on the wall of the art teacher Lake's studio contain figures with identical facial ex-pressions, although one picture is a photograph and one is a re-production of the head of Christ from a Rembrandt drawing. Similarly, the paintings of the sentimental émigré artist Gram-ineev closely resemble the photographs taken by Mira Beloch-kin, Pnin's Russian sweetheart. Gramineev was a "well-known, frankly academic painter, whose soulful oils—'Mother Volga,' 'Three Old Friends' (lad, nag, dog), 'April Glade,' and so forth— still graced a museum in Moscow" (p. 127). Some of Mira's "ar-tistic snapshots" are of the same subjects: "pets, clouds, flowers, an April glade . . . , a sunset skyline, a hand holding a book" (pp. 133–34). The painter, the sunset skyline in Mira's photo-graph, and the actual people surrounding Pnin in the present eventually merge into an image in which even the narrator can-not, or will not, separate the real from the contrived: "On the distant crest of the knoll, at the exact spot where Gramineev's easel had stood a few hours before, two dark figures in profile were silhouetted against the ember-red sky. They stood there closely, facing each other. One could not make out from the road whether it was the Poroshin girl and her beau, or Nina Bolotov and young Poroshin, or merely an emblematic couple placed with easy art on the last page of Pnin's fading day" (p. 136).

The two clearest examples of the merging of art and actuality are Laurence Clements's discovery of an exact likeness of him-self in Jan van Eyck's painting of Canon van der Paele, and Jack Cockerell's imitation of Pnin. Cockerell has worked at his perfor-mance so long and so successfully that not only can he imper-sonate Pnin to perfection, he has also in the process "acquired an unmistakable resemblance to the man he had now been mimicking for almost ten years" (p. 187). Hidden in the names of these two characters, Clements and Cockerell, are allusions to two plays by Arthur Schnitzler, author of *Libelei*, the play the narrator recalls seeing Pnin perform in back in 1916. Clements takes his name from the character Clemens in *Literature*, and Cockerell (whose wife is named Gwen) takes his from the title of *The Green Cockatoo*. Both plays share themes with *Pnin*, since both are about the impossibility of distinguishing between what Schnitzler calls "pretense" and "truth." *Literature* contains a very Liza-like character named Margaret who writes (as Liza does) bad love poetry. Her fiance, Clemens, objects to Margaret's aspirations as a writer on the grounds that the poet or novelist is an emotional exhibitionist who shamelessly exposes his most intimate secrets to the public gaze. Margaret retorts that the writer does not always tell the truth: "We write of things we've never experienced, things we've dreamed or only invented."[4] By the end of the play, however, it has become clear that Margaret's novel is in fact a true account of her life—which has been a series of carefully contrived gestures designed to make good material for a novel. In this sense, Margaret's novel tells the truth, and her life tells a lie.

The Green Cockatoo is set in Paris on July 14, 1789—the day the Bastille was stormed. A cafe owner has discovered that he can attract a wealthy aristocratic clientele to his cafe by hiring down-and-out actors to pose as exaggerated versions of themselves for the entertainment of the customers. As part of their act, they boast that the day is soon coming when they and their audience will have exchanged places. When news reaches the cafe that the Bastille has been taken and that members of the government are being killed, the audience is thrown into confusion, not knowing whether they are still watching a performance or not. The import of all this confusion is summarized by one member of the audience, the poet Rollin: "Reality—acting—can you always tell the difference, Chevalier? . . . I cannot—and what I find so remarkable here is that the apparent differences are done away with. Truth dissolves into pretense, pretense into truth."[5]

The apparent differences are also done away with in *Pnin*, so that it is ultimately impossible to determine how much of the narrator's account of Timofey Pnin is "truth" and how much is

pretense. Even when he seems most honest and straightfor-
ward, relating an event he himself has witnessed, his perspective frames the event and his imagination colors it, so that what
we are given is always an image compounded of reality and
imagination. At the end of the novel, for example, the narrator
describes his last glimpse of his "good friend" Pnin. By an especially cruel twist of fate's knife, the narrator has been hired to fill
the vacancy created at Waindell by the firing of Pnin; he is to
launch his career there with a public lecture. Arriving in town a
day early, he spends the night with the Cockerells and is treated
to a great deal of Scotch and the famous impersonation. This
drunken hilarity at Pnin's expense leaves the narrator with "the
mental counterpart of a bad taste in the mouth" (p. 189); he
sleeps badly and slips out early the next morning in search of
breakfast. In the course of his walk he spots Pnin speeding out
of Waindell, all his possessions and the stray dog he couldn't
leave behind loaded into the car: "From where I stood I watched
them recede in the frame of the roadway, between the Moorish
house and the Lombardy poplar. Then the little sedan boldly
swung past the front truck and, free at last, spurted up the shining road, which one could make out narrowing to a thread of
gold in the soft mist where hill after hill made beauty of distance,
and where there was simply no saying what miracle might happen" (p. 191).

Pnin, who has lost his job to a rival and had to give up his
beloved house on Todd Road, who has absolutely no place to
go, and whose departure is of interest only to Cockerell, who
wanted one more chance to mock Pnin with a drunken midnight
serenade, thus departs in a framed picture, up a golden road
into the soft mist of a future of miraculous possibilities. One
clear sign, then, of how much manipulating the narrator is up to
in this passage is that there is simply no way to justify its rosy—
or golden—optimism. But there are other signs of the made-up
quality of the entire passage that appear when we pay close attention to the details of the scene.

Most readers have seen little irony in this concluding passage,
finding instead that it "evokes and affirms Pnin's continued vitality"; that it is a sign of Pnin's having sloughed off his roles of
exile and alien to become a kind of existential hero, "the man,

free and at home in his homelessness"; that even in this passage
the narrator "does not appear to be a distorting refractor of the
events he relates"; or that the narrator's dismissal of Pnin is a
positive moral choice, a sign of his refusal to play the Pninian
role of victim.[6] Other readers have described Pnin's departure as
a successful flight from the prying of the narrator,[7] and certainly
this is a logical explanation of why Pnin chooses to leave early in
the morning of the very day—Pnin's birthday, incidentally—he
expects the narrator to arrive in Waindell. But the framed picture is not of a defeated man in flight; it is of a confident adven-
turer setting out to seek the fortune that lies just beyond those
lovely hills. The narrator's description of Pnin's departure is very
similar to the account of Chichikov's departure from the town of
N—— in Gogol's *Dead Souls*. (I might note that the narrator is
accompanied on his early morning walk by a four-footed clue—
the Cockerell's dog Sobakevich, who shares his name, which
means "son of a bitch" in Russian, with a character in *Dead
Souls*.) As Chichikov speeds out of town, "everything is flying
by: the mileposts fly, merchants fly by on the boxes of their car-
riages . . . ; the entire highway is flying none knows whither
away into the dissolving distance" (*Gogol*, p. 111). Nabokov's
comment on this lyrical passage, and I have quoted from his
translation of it, is suggestive: "Beautiful as all this final cre-
scendo sounds, it is from the stylistic point of view merely a conjuror's patter enabling an object to disappear, the particular
object being—Chichikov" (*Gogol*, p. 113). Pnin's exit, like Chichikov's, is a matter of style, the narrator's dismissal of the Pnin he
has created.[8]

While we know very little about this narrator, what we do
know suggests that in several important respects he and Pnin
are opposites, and that in filling in the outlines of Pnin's personality he has attributed to Pnin the very qualities he lacks himself.
Early in the novel he indicates that he is a realist with a strong
streak of pessimism: "Some people—and I am one of them—
hate happy ends. We feel cheated. Harm is the norm. Doom
should not jam. The avalanche stopping in its tracks a few feet
above the cowering village behaves not only unnaturally but un-
ethically. Had I been reading about this mild old man, instead of
writing about him . . ." (pp. 25–26). But he *is* writing about

Pnin the incurable romantic, creating out of the things that distress him a faintly absurd character who nevertheless is able to
cope with those very sources of distress. His anxieties grow out
of his consciousness of what Van Veen calls "the direction of
Time, the ardis of Time, one-way Time, . . . the irreversibility of
Time" (*Ada*, p. 573). The narrator is on the one hand tormented
by the inexorable backward glide of all things into the past; in
recalling his childhood visit to Pnin's father (an eye specialist) to
have a speck removed from his eye, he wonders "where that
speck is now? The dull, mad fact is that it *does* exist somewhere"
(p. 176). On the other hand, he visualizes the only future await-
ing all living things as "a kind of soundlessly spinning ethereal
void" (p. 69).

Out of this anxiety he creates Pnin, a man for whom all that is
most dear has been buried in the past and whose faulty heart
should keep him constantly aware of the proximity of death, yet
who is so undisturbed by the passage of time that he never even
takes note of his own birthday. Pnin has several defenses against
despair at the treasonableness of time. One is his spontaneous
and unabashed delight in living: "He was alive and that was sufficient" (p. 24). His psychological resilience is strong enough to
defeat the efforts of his treacherous hearts (the real one and the
metaphoric one) to lead him into despair—sufficient even to
save him from his hopeless, suffocating love for Liza. "If people
are reunited in Heaven," Pnin muses, "(I don't believe it, but
suppose), then how shall I stop it from creeping upon me, over
me, that shriveled, helpless, lame thing, her soul? But this is the
earth, and I am, curiously enough, alive, and there is something
in me and in life—" (p. 58). Pnin is interrupted before he can
complete this thought by an urgent request: a thirsty squirrel is
asking him to turn on the water fountain. Pnin accedes to this
demand as naturally as he accedes to the more difficult demands
that life—and Liza—make on him. He keeps the fountain on
long enough for the squirrel to drink its fill; then, "its thirst
quenched, the squirrel departed without the least sign of gratitude" (p. 58). Liza too has just departed from Pnin without a
sign of gratitude, after having secured his assent to *her* urgent
request that he send her son Victor some money each month.

Joan Clements, the most sympathetic and sensible of the secondary characters in the book, is used on occasion as a convenient, reliable mouthpiece for the narrator. After Liza's brief visit to Waindell, which finally convinces Pnin that he has lost her forever, Joan attempts to distract the disconsolate Timofey by showing him magazine pictures. She tries to interest him in a cartoon drawing of a desert island with palm tree, shipwrecked sailor, and mermaid, but Pnin refuses to be amused:

"Impossible," said Pnin. "So small island, moreover with palm, cannot exist in such big sea."
"Well, it exists here."
"Impossible isolation," said Pnin.
"Yes, but—Really, you are not playing fair, Timofey. You know perfectly well you agree with Lore that the world of the mind is based on a compromise with logic." [P. 60]

Joan's homiletic remark contains one of those puns that the practiced reader of Nabokov learns not to overlook. "Lore" is her nickname for her philosopher husband Laurence, but the word also suggests the "paradise of Russian lore" (p. 73) that is Pnin's refuge and chief delight as a scholar, and the source of material for his book. This kind of lore makes its own compromise with logic and with the sterile facts and chronologies of history.

The events of the recent past have confirmed Pnin's belief that "the history of man is the history of pain" (p. 168). But the *grande histoire* that records human pain is only half the story; Pnin's *petite histoire* will tell the other half. His book will complete the sentence that Pnin began, at a moment when he was feeling acutely the painfulness of his own life: "But this is the earth, and I am, curiously enough, alive, and there is something in me and in life—" (p. 58). (A similar situation occurs in *Ada*; there Van Veen writes a very long book to complete one of Ada's similes.) Pnin's alternative history will document man's persistent, irrational belief that harm is not the norm, that doom will eventually jam. The lore that fascinates Pnin—like the Green Week ceremony he reads about in a book on Russian myth, still practiced "in the margins of Christian ritual" (p. 77) in the nineteenth century, in which peasant maidens floated wreaths of spring flowers on the Volga—is a celebration of continuity, recurrence, and eternal return.[9] Pnin himself, in spite of the fact that each new year seems to bring new losses and new disappointments, still can look forward eagerly to the "springtime splendor, all honey and hum" (p. 145), of the lilacs in his yard. When Pnin discovers his Green Week maidens he immediately associates them with Shakespeare's Ophelia; the folk ceremony, Shakespeare's fictions, and the narrator's inventive history of Pnin are all artificial, stylized forms—art forms, in short—which preserve the kind of irrational, subjective truths, verifiable only by the strength of their attraction on human thought and feeling, that offer an alternative to the historian's approximations.

Pnin has another saving quality which the narrator lacks, the ability to relinquish fully those things that are irretrievably lost and to delight in the novelty of the replacements that are provided. Pnin is, as Yeats says all men are, in love and loves what vanishes. The most valuable of the many things Pnin has "lost, dumped, shed" (p. 19) is the beloved Russia of his youth. Rather than remaining an exile mourning his homelessness, however, Pnin, after a transitional interval in Paris, chooses a new home— "America, my new country, wonderful America which sometimes surprises me but always provokes respect" (p. 104). Pnin is even willing to make difficult concessions to his new country, struggling with its unwieldy language and consenting to be called "Tim" rather than the "Timofey Pavlovich" he prefers. When he has to have all his teeth pulled, Pnin spends the first few toothless days "in mourning for an intimate part of himself. It surprised him to realize how fond he had been of his teeth." But once he gets his false teeth, Pnin characteristically stops regretting and rejoices in his discovery of something new, even if it is a substitute for the beloved original. Suddenly the new gadget, his plate, is "a revelation, it was a sunrise, it was a firm mouthful of efficient, alabastrine, humane America" (p. 38).

The Russia that Pnin loved died in the civil war of 1918–22. In the America of the 1950s Pnin is surrounded by evidence of the residue left by the turmoil of Russia's recent past: McCarthyism; his intellectual émigré friends, liberals and libertarians in prerevolutionary Russia, who now belong to American anticommunist organizations; the Starrs' modish interest in Dostoevski and Shostakovich; President Poore's charitable commencement-speech reference to "Russia—the country of Tolstoy, Stanislavski, Raskolnikov, and other great and good men" (p. 136); the student who hopes after a semester of Russian grammar to be able to read *Anna Karamazov* in the original; the 1940s Russian propaganda film including shots of a happy worker's family and the unanimous nomination of Stalin as candidate from the Stalin Election District of Moscow. These attitudes and postures underscore the isolation of the greatest and most apolitical Slavophile of them all, Timofey Pnin, for whom Russia is a wrenching memory of things he loved and has lost—parents, friends, the beautiful Mira Belochkin, and the birches and bird cherries of the Russian woods.

Pnin has trained himself not to think of these things too often, but he has moments when time collapses for him, when something in the present brings the past back in an unexpected rush, so that Pnin for a moment lives simultaneously in the past and the present. The park between Waindell and Cremona, with its rhododendrons and oaks, brings back a childhood delirium in which he became obsessed with the pattern of rhododendron and oak on the wallpaper of his room; facing the audience at the Cremona Women's Club brings back an evening on which schoolboy Pnin recited a Pushkin poem before an audience that included his parents and Mira Belochkin; watching and listening to his Russian friends gathered for tea on the porch of Al Cook's country house brings back an evening in the summer of 1916 when he and Mira met in the garden while their families had tea on the porch of the Belochkins' country house.

These visions that come upon Pnin unexpectedly fuse past and present into a single image which juxtaposes the banality of Pnin's current surroundings with memories of the most intensely felt experiences of his past. In the few moments before he begins delivering his address to the Cremona Women's Club, for example, Pnin sees his audience undergo a strange transformation:

In the middle of the front row of seats he saw one of his Baltic aunts. . . . Next to her, shyly smiling, sleek dark head inclined, gentle brown gaze shining up at Pnin from under velvet eyebrows, sat a dead sweetheart of his, fanning herself with a program. Murdered, forgotten, unrevenged, incorrupt, immortal, many old friends were scattered throughout the dim hall among more recent people, such as Miss Clyde, who had modestly regained a front seat. Vanya Bednyashkin, shot by the Reds in 1919 in Odessa because his father had been a Liberal, was gaily signaling to his former schoolmate from the back of the hall. And in an inconspicuous situation Dr. Pavel Pnin and his anxious wife, both a little blurred but on the whole wonderfully recovered from their obscure dissolution, looked at their son with the same life-consuming passion and pride that they had looked at him with that night in 1912 when, at a school festival, commemorating Napoleon's defeat, he had recited (a bespectacled lad all alone on the stage) a poem by Pushkin.

The brief vision was gone. Old Miss Herring, retired Professor of History, author of *Russia Awakes* (1922), was bending across one or two intermediate members of the audience to compliment Miss Clyde on her speech, while from behind that lady another twinkling old party was thrusting into her field of vision a pair of withered, soundlessly clapping hands. [Pp. 27–28]

The mention of old Miss Herring and her book on Russia is not gratuitous; the images stored in Pnin's unconscious memory, this passage suggests, give a truer and more resonant picture of the past than the historian's chronicle of events and movements can give.

Proust says of the personal past that "it is a labour in vain to attempt to recapture it: all the efforts of our intellect must prove futile. The past is hidden somewhere outside the realm, beyond the reach of intellect." [10] The narrator of *Pnin*, who once boasts of "the unusual lucidity and strength of my memory" (pp. 179–80), becomes confused in his recollections of actual events in the past because his memory is an effort of the intellect, subverted by his anxieties about the past. For example, the guilt he apparently feels for his part in bringing about Pnin's marriage to Liza causes him to misremember Pnin's part in the performance of *Libelei*. He recalls that Pnin took the part of the cuckolded husband who avenges himself by killing his wife's young lover in a duel; Pnin, on the other hand, insists that he played the part of the old father who is left alone and distraught at the end of the play when his daughter leaves him, apparently to commit suicide. Paradoxically, we are by the end of the novel convinced of the reliability of Pnin, who is largely a creature of the narrator's imagination, and of the unreliability of the narrator who creates him. Like Schnitzler's Margaret, the narrator fabricates, with the aid of imagination, a convincing fictive truth out of the approximations and half-truths of the real.

The narrator's subject, Timofey Pnin, is also his model.[11] Like Pnin's work on Old Russia, the narrator's book about Pnin is a commentary that serves as a necessary adjunct to the "real" life. While we grant the fictiveness of the narrator's account, we also recognize that it is no less "true" than Pnin's *petite histoire*; both define a life—one the life of a country, the other the life of a man—in terms of its texture, rather than in terms of a series of actions. In both instances those actions provide the text, but it is the commentary that gives the text authenticity, authority, and meaning.

Six

Ada or Ardor:
A Family Chronicle

Ada is the most lush, the most exuberant, the most playful, the most allusive, the most erotic, and clearly the most ambitious of Nabokov's novels in English. In sheer scope *Ada* is the "biggest" of the novels, as befits a family chronicle. It is also the most egregiously fantastic, in that not only are the book's people invented but the very planet they inhabit is a fiction. More important, *Ada* is the most ambitious and explicit treatment of a number of themes that have been at least implicit in all the previous novels: the loss of the fragile Eden of childhood and the banality of the failed Edens of the present; the relationship between art and time, especially between art and memory; the capacity of the imagination to deepen and enrich one's experience of the actual world; the final impossibility of knowing as incontestably "real" anything but one's own most intensely felt experiences. Above all, *Ada*, both as Van Veen's memoir and Nabokov's novel, affirms the value of art as a way of overcoming the rigidity of chronological sequence, which separates past and present and makes the past final, changeless, and irretrievably lost.

The narrator of this memoir-novel, Van Veen, becomes a writer almost by default. His first book is undertaken in part as a way of compensating for his failing athletic abilities—the substitution, in effect, of one kind of exhibitionism for another. Van's greatest athletic triumph as a young man is his ability to walk on his hands with astonishing grace and agility. He is so good at it, in fact, that for a short while he becomes a professional performer, billing himself as Mascodagama, wearing an elaborate costume, and amazing his audiences by doing the tango on his hands as easily as he did it on his feet. Writing about it much later, Van says of his Mascodagama performance that it was "an oversophisticated parody of his own act" (p. 194). The description applies equally well to Nabokov's novel: *Ada* is a sophisticated, hyperbolic, and very elaborate staging of some of Nabokov's most familiar acts.

Interestingly, the other Nabokov book which *Ada* most closely resembles is the autobiography, *Speak, Memory*. Like *Ada* it is a "systematically correlated assemblage of personal recollections" which has at its center the story of a young writer's first love and his attempts to "recapture the miracle of its initial moments, the rustle and rush of those limes in the rain, the compassion of the wild countryside" (*Speak, Memory*, pp. 9, 238). The index to *Speak, Memory* suggests how close the two books are in texture and tone. Of the 277 items in the index, 243 are proper names. The remaining 34 items read like a subject index to *Ada*: Bicycling, Brothers, Butterflies (see Lepidoptera), caterpillars (see Lepidoptera), Colored hearing (see also Stained glass), Dachshunds, Drawings, Father, Jewels (see also Stained glass), Lepidoptera, Mother, Moths (see Lepidoptera), Mushrooms, Poem, Stained glass (see also Jewels and Pavilion), Trains, and so on. Such an overlapping between the autobiography and the novel is not necessarily surprising, since we might expect a novelist to incorporate into his fiction the things that he knows and cares about most. It is the method of their incorporation that is interesting and that offers important insights into what both books have to say about the uses of memory.

The butterflies and jewels and stained glass of *Speak, Memory* are combined and recombined into patterns which provide the structural framework of the memoir, patterns that shake themselves loose from time and space constraints, sometimes flagrantly and sometimes almost imperceptibly. Nabokov's discussion of his early passion for butterflies, for example, ends with the description of a July day on which he set out with his net from the banks of the Oredezh River near his family's Vyra estate, outside Saint Petersburg. The young collector passes through a marsh teeming with moths and bog orchids and emerges, on the same magic day, at the foot of Longs Peak in Colorado, where an older Nabokov hunted butterflies years later:

I pursued rose-margined Sulphurs, gray-marbled Satyrs. Unmindful of the mosquitoes that furred my forearms, I stooped with a grunt of delight to snuff out the life of some silver-studded lepidopteron throbbing in the folds of my net.
Through the smells of the bog, I caught the subtle perfume of butterfly wings on my fingers, a perfume which varies with the species—vanilla, or lemon, or musk, or a musty, sweetish odor difficult to define. Still unsated, I pressed forward. At last I saw I had come to the end of the marsh. The rising ground beyond was a paradise of lupines, columbines, and pentstemons. Mariposa lilies bloomed under Ponderosa pines. In the distance, fleeting cloud shadows dappled the dull green of slopes above timber line, and the gray and white of Longs Peak. [*Speak, Memory*, pp. 138–39]

Memory, even a memoirist's memory, may not be faithful to times and places, but it is always faithful to the sounds, colors, and smells of intensely felt experience. These sensory memories form a single timeless image, a "magic carpet [folded], after use, in such a way as to superimpose one part of the pattern upon another" (*Speak, Memory*, p. 139). The gradual piecing together of that pattern is the subject of both *Ada* and *Speak, Memory*.[1]

Ada is also a memoir, a commentary on his own life begun by Van Veen at the age of eighty-seven and never completed. Like *Speak, Memory* it is a tribute to the "supreme achievement of memory, which is the masterly use it makes of innate harmonies when gathering to its fold the suspended and wandering tonalities of the past" (*Speak, Memory*, p. 126). But *Ada* is also—and more importantly—a tribute to the supreme achievement of art, which can shape, preserve, and protect those recollected harmonies. The *Ada* we read is, presumably, an edition of that bound copy of the typed, supposedly complete manuscript which Van's secretary presented to him on his ninety-seventh birthday and which was "immediately blotted out by a regular inferno of alterations in red ink and blue pencil" (p. 624)—the blue pencil belonging to Van, the red pen to Ada. While we cannot know what changes were made in the body of the manuscript (although we do know that part 5 was added), the marginal notes and annotations of Van and Ada have been duly noted by the editor and incorporated into the text, conveniently freeing the margins which Van and Ada, given longer to live, would surely have filled with more scholia. As long as Van and Ada are alive, the clean manuscript copy of the memoir represents only a specious perfection, since they are by living both enlarging and altering the subject of the commentary—their common past.

Van and Ada delight in recalling their past, even while they are still young enough to have little of it to recall. The phrase "and do you remember" becomes a standard device in their conversation, Van notes, almost from the beginning. But as the stored mass of accumulated memories grows it becomes more shapeless and its chronology becomes increasingly difficult to sort out. Did the Burning Barn episode come before or after the discovery of Marina's diary in the loft? On which occasion was Ada wearing her black blazer? Memory fades quickly, but imagination (as Van observes) does not. The commentary is an attempt to preserve the past as it is remade by the imagination—a past pieced together out of impressions, sensations, dreams, and whatever scraps of fact remain. In one of those incidental details, frequently found in Nabokov's novels, which have little to do with the book's story but a great deal to do with its themes, Van mentions that his favorite novel is one entitled *The Slat Sign*. The exact meaning of that curious title is difficult to pin down; fortunately, Nabokov used the phrase in another place, and this time the context suggests its appropriateness to *Ada*. Responding to Herbert Gold's recollections of their friendship, Nabokov observes in his *Anniversary Notes* that Gold is "blending fact and fiction in a kind of slat-sign shimmer" (*Strong Opinions*, p. 298). That kind of blending is precisely the function of memory and art as they work in *Ada* to preserve the past as a collection of shimmering, sensuous images.

As the account of his virtually lifelong love affair with his sister, Van's book is a kind of ode on intimations of mortality, a hard-earned recognition of the necessary devolution of poetic sublimity into prosaic banality. The affair begins in the edenic arbors of Ardis, the family estate; Van and Ada are young, innocent, and awed by the splendors of their fresh green world— including their own splendidly energetic eroticism. (Their first kiss occurs, appropriately, in the branches of a tree imported to Ardis from the Eden National Park.) The promises of this auspicious and unblemished first summer, however, cannot be kept; the serpents in their particular Eden come in droves. During her absences from Van, Ada is pursued by a series of suitors, all of whom she submits to, partly out of sympathy and partly because, as she tells Van, he had "let loose something mad in me when we were only children, a physical hankering, an insatiable itch" (p. 354). The result for Van is jealous rage which drives him away from Ada in a fury, even though he is a victim of the same itch and has assuaged it much more often than Ada has.[2]

Van is fairly indiscriminate in his amours, with one exception; his and Ada's half-sister Lucette loves him as ardently as Ada does, but Van (unlike his father, Demon) refuses to use the vulnerable sister as a surrogate for the stronger, prouder woman he loves. Lucette is driven to suicide by the hopelessness of her love for Van, and her death jolts Van and Ada into a new awareness of just how far behind they have left their innocent paradise. Their grief is given a sharper edge by the guilt they both feel for not having recognized that Lucette's emotional needs could be as imperious, as much a matter of life and death, as their own. "We never learned in the arbors of Ardis," Ada says, "that such unhappiness could exist" (p. 531). There are other difficult distractions besides lust, jealousy, and guilt waiting for Van and Ada outside the walled garden of Ardis—such as the strong social and moral proscriptions against incest. At first these taboos only enforce the delicious privacy of the love affair, but when Demon eventually discovers what is actually going on between his children he argues against the alliance in terms strong enough to send the lovers off in opposite directions, Van into wandering, nearly suicidal despair and Ada into a convenient marriage with an American rancher.

All these problems require difficult adjustments and the patience to wait until death has removed the people who stand in the way (especially their parents, Demon and Marina), yet none of them is finally insurmountable. Time is on the side of Van and Ada in this respect, but, ironically, time also turns out to be the most potent of the serpents in paradise, the one enemy that will not die and refuses to be bought off or beaten into submission. When Van and Ada are finally free and the remaining minor impediments can be relegated, as Van believes, to "a few last pages of epilogical mopping up far away from the reality of *their* united lives" (p. 561), they are shocked to find just how much they have lost to time. Ada, now fifty, only faintly resembles the twelve-year-old child Van first fell in love with:

She wore a corset which stressed the unfamiliar stateliness of her body enveloped in a black-velvet gown of a flowing cut both eccentric and monastic, as their mother used to favor. . . . She made lavish use of cosmetics to camouflage the lines at the outer corners of her fat carmined lips and dark-shadowed eyes whose opaque iris now seemed less mysterious than myopic owing to the nervous flutter of her painted lashes. . . . Nothing remained of her gangling grace, and the new mellowness, and the velvet stuff, had an irritatingly dignified air of obstacle and defense. . . . At their earlier reunions the constraint, subsisting as a dull ache after the keen agonies of Fate's surgery, used to be soon drowned in sexual desire, leaving life to pick up by and by. Now they were on their own. [Pp. 592–93]

Although Van and Ada are now unencumbered, wealthy, and still very much in love, the Eden of their remaining life together is so diminished as to barely resemble that first paradise of Ardis. They must now contend with the distressing and degrading realities of age: the gradual loss of the physical desire that had in the beginning been the keenest of love's pleasures; the increasing discomforts of illness and pain; and the terrifying knowledge of approaching death.

Van's book is largely an account of his reconciliation to these diminishments and his discovery of the only agent capable of confounding time—his writing. The long opening section of the book, which describes the wonders of the first summer at Ardis, was written partly in response to two earlier accounts of that summer. The first of these is the series of photographs taken by the blackmailing kitchen boy, Kim Beauharnais. The second account is contained in the rumors-turned-legends that sprang up in the countryside around Ardis, propagated and sustained by a chorus of characters appropriate to a romantic idyll:

Romantically inclined handmaids, whose reading consisted of *Gwen de Vere* and *Klara Mertvago*, adored Van, adored Ada, adored Ardis's ardors in arbors. Their swains, plucking ballads on their seven-stringed Russian lyres under the racemosa in bloom or in old rose gardens (while the windows went out one by one in the castle), added freshly composed lines—naive, lackey-daisical, but heartfelt—to cyclic folk songs. Eccentric police officers grew enamored with the glamour of incest. Gardeners paraphrased iridescent Persian poems about irrigation and the Four Arrows of Love. Nightwatchmen fought insomnia and the fire of the clap with the weapons of *Vaniada's Adventures*. Herdsmen, spared by thunderbolts on remote hillsides, used their huge "moaning horns" as ear trumpets to catch the lilts of Ladore. Virgin châtelaines in marble-floored manors fondled their lone flames fanned by Van's romance. And another century would pass, and the painted word would be retouched by the still richer brush of time. [P. 433]

Van's account falls somewhere in the middle, between the stark realism of the photographs and the muzzy sentimentality of the legends; it blends fact and myth, the actual and the imaginary, into a version of the truth that is more intensely felt as "real" than its components taken alone could be.[3] His account also redeems the past and keeps it alive, in ways that these other accounts cannot do, by merging it with the present, collapsing both into a timeless pattern of experience that preserves "the meaningful richness of color and contour in an otherwise meaningless vision" (p. 264).

The multiple worlds of *Ada* and its people tempt the reader to look for a neat scheme or diagram, like the Veen family tree, that would make the complexity and diversity of the novel more manageable. That is, the reader's impulse is to make the Terra and Antiterra of the novel *stand* for something and to see a parable in this story of incest that ends, if not happily, at least contentedly. But any scheme of that sort, like the Veen family tree, does not stand up to a close look. We know for certain that the family tree hides the truth about Van and Ada's kinship, and there are hints in the novel—and in the genealogy itself—that this diagram hides other indiscretions, perhaps even other instances of incest. Any schematic reading of *Ada* would be just as deceptive; behind its fancies are clusters of allusions and echoes of many other fancies, and what really matters is not what they might represent but the ways in which they impinge on each other and coalesce into the vision of this book, this "Organized Dream" (p. 369).

To be more specific: the many pairs, doubles, twins, and look-alikes in *Ada*, including the look-alike planets Terra and Antiterra, are reflections of that double nature of experience, and the kind of split vision it makes necessary, that Nabokov has written about before, most notably in *Lolita* and *Pale Fire*. In the world according to Nabokov, fascination and even significance are largely a matter of resemblance, or looking alike. A simple thing seen in isolation may be momentarily interesting, but when a complex thing is seen together with its mimotype, there is room for an entire world of wonders in the slight asymmetry between the two. Even if such resemblances are coincidental, they have the intrinsic interest of the surprise of any unlooked-for overlapping, and they also raise the possibility of fixing, as Van suggests, the "number of coincidences, in a given domain, after which they cease to be coincidences, and form, instead, the living organism of a new truth" (p. 383). But if resemblances are *not* coincidental, then they can be seen as endlessly fascinating clues to a grand design, calculated moves in the intricate game of worlds.

The list of specifically paired people and things in *Ada* is long; it includes Terra and Antiterra, Van and Ada, Ada and Lucette, Demon and Dan, Aqua and Marina, art and science, heaven and hell—Ada's name is Russian for "hell," and as she points out, "there's a Van in Nirvana" (p. 620)—past and present, love and lust—the "rose and the sore" of Eros (p. 389). (The names of Terra and Antiterra suggest Eros and Anteros, the paired mythological figures frequently used by Renaissance artists to represent the physical and spiritual aspects of love. In fact, some of the most famous renderings of the two Cupids were done by a Dutch artist with the interesting name of Otho van Veen.) In most of these cases the exact relationship between the two parts of the pair is obscure. Demon and Dan, for instance, are described as cousins, and their places on the family tree bear out this description. Yet it seems suspicious that they were born on the same day and that Demon is said to be of "Anglo-Irish" ancestry, while the only English name given in the genealogy is that of Dan's mother, Mary Trumbell, and the only specifically Irish name is that of Aqua and Marina's grandmother, Mary O'Reilly. It seems possible that Demon and Dan are actually twin brothers (even possible that they are the twin brothers or half-brothers of Aqua and Marina) who pose as cousins (as Van and Ada do) for the sake of family respectability—but that remains only a possibility; the Veen family tree refuses to yield all its secrets. There are other puzzles that are never solved, such as the identity of the child who was born and buried at the time of Van's birth, at Ex en Valais. Van refers to this child as "my stillborn double" (p. 376); Demon and Marina are silent on the subject, and mad Aqua, who believes that Van is her son, at times confuses him with "a stillborn male infant half a year old, a surprised little fetus, a fish of rubber that she had produced in her bath, in a *lieu de naissance* plainly marked X in her dreams" (p. 28). Was this stillborn child Aqua's, or did Marina bear one live twin and one dead one?

If the muddled relationships among the members of the Veen family are finally impossible to sort out, so is the exact relationship between the two worlds of *Ada*—the actual world of Antiterra and the possible world of Terra. The most interesting aspect of the continuing dispute on Antiterra over the existence of the other world is that the grounds of the debate are always philosophical and psychological; scientific investigations are, apparently, irrelevant to the question. In fact, belief in the physical existence of Terra is taken on Antiterra as one of the symptoms (or causes) of insanity: "minds *bien rangés* (not apt to unhobble hobgoblins), rejected Terra as a fad or fantom, and deranged minds (ready to plunge into any abyss) accepted it in support and token of their own irrationality" (p. 20). Differences of opinion among investigators of the subject—all of them sane, presumably—seem to be matters of sensibility only; Van remarks that even the most eminent researchers were "emotionally divided" on the question of the existence of Terra (p. 20).

Another curious fact about Terra is that, like some of Nabokov's narrators, it loses its discrete identity through a sly narrational twist at the end of the book. Elderly Van and Ada are incensed to find that Van's first book and only novel, *Letters from Terra*, has been turned into a preposterous science-fiction movie. What angers them most are the liberties that the director, Victor Vitry, has taken in presenting Terra's historical background. This "absurdly farfetched" (p. 617) history of Terra turns out to be a caricatured but essentially accurate summary of the history of our own familiar planet in the twentieth century. Despite Van's insistence that this version of Terra is a distortion and a hoax, the film is an overnight box-office success, and the implications of its universal popularity are, to Van's amazement, revolutionary:

From the tremendous correspondence that piled up on Van's desk during a few years of world fame, one gathered that thousands of more or less unbalanced people believed (so striking was the visual impact of the Vitry-Veen film) in the secret Government-concealed identity of Terra and Antiterra. Demonian reality dwindled to a casual illusion. Actually, we had passed through all that. Politicians, dubbed Old Felt and Uncle Joe in forgotten comics, had really existed. Tropical countries meant, not only Wild Nature Reserves but famine, and death, and ignorance, and shamans, and agents from distant Atomsk. Our world *was*, in fact, mid-twentieth century. [P. 618]

In the film, the force of visual images is sufficient to turn speculation into fact and to allow an entire history of the world to spring, full blown, into being. Similarly, in Van's narrative, Terra and Antiterra are merged, by absolute fiat, in the course of a single, understated, ambiguous paragraph.

The fusion of the actual world and the imagined one at the

end of Van Veen's memoir is very much like the merging of "mirage and reality" that is the subject of Humbert Humbert's confessions and of Charles Kinbote's annotations. All three of these
narrators, in fact, find themselves most at home in a neutral territory like the one Hawthorne described in his "Customs House"
sketch, located "somewhere between the real world and fairy-
land, where the Actual and the Imaginary may meet, and each
imbue itself with the nature of the other."[4] Hawthorne's neutral
territory was a small, strange place—his working example was a
silent room at midnight, illuminated by the transfiguring light of
the moon—reserved for the special kind of narrative art that he
called romance. In Nabokov's fiction, on the other hand, this
same territory has become the province of all art, and the boundaries of Hawthorne's darkened room have been extended to include the entire multicolored world we know and whatever
other worlds we might dream of or fear or wish for. There is another important difference between Hawthorne's neutral territory and Nabokov's: for the narrators of Nabokov's books, including *Speak, Memory*, the "fairy-land" they set in opposition to
the "real world" is the very private world of their own past, a
place that is always partly remembered and partly imagined.
That fantastic world is, ironically, much less exotic and disorienting to them than the actuality of the immediate present. For
these narrators, then, the problem they face is the one Demon
Veen dismisses as a "logical impossibility": how to "relate the
dubious reality of the present to the unquestionable one of remembrance" (p. 265).

Van Veen, who is by avocation a philosopher of time, stumbles onto the solution to Demon's logical impossibility in an epi-
phanic moment that both he and the reader recognize as the
true climax of his book.* ("After the glory of the summit," Van
says of this moment, "there came the difficult descent" [p. 592].)
Having devoted years of research and thought to the problem of
how to establish continuity between past and present, Van suddenly finds that the simple solution has sneaked up on him un-

---

*Interestingly, Nabokov's conception of the novel apparently began with what
is now its climactic scene. He once spoke of this scene as the "springboard"
which allowed the rest of the novel to "leap into the kind of existence that can
and must be put into words" (*Strong Opinions*, p. 122).

awares. The catalytic agent is a telephone call from Ada, whom he has not seen or spoken to for seventeen years:

> Now it so happened that she had never—never, at least, in adult life—spoken to him by phone; hence the phone had preserved the very essence, the bright vibration, of her vocal cords, the little "leap" in her larynx, the laugh clinging to the contour of the phrase, as if afraid in girlish glee to slip off the quick words it rode. It was the timbre of their past, as if the past had put through that call, a miraculous connection. . . .
>
> That telephone voice, by resurrecting the past and linking it up with the present, with the darkening slate-blue mountains beyond the lake, with the spangles of the sun wake dancing through the poplar, formed the centerpiece in his deepest perception of tangible time, the glittering "now" that was the only reality of Time's texture. [Pp. 591–92]

This description of the linkage of past and present in a moment of pure, isolated time that transcends chronological distinctions has a decidedly Proustian quality—as, in fact, does much of *Ada*. The framing devices of this novel and Proust's, for example, are identical: at the end of *Ada* Van and Ada are discovered to be writing the very book we are reading, and it becomes clear that the rest of the book has been a preparation, as it is in Proust's novel, for this act of creation with which the book ends. Both novels are about memory and art, about the ability of unconscious memory to preserve in sensuous images those things which have been lost to the conscious memory. But there are important differences between Nabokov's conception of past time and Proust's; in musing about the nature of time, Van warns himself to beware "the marcel wave of fashionable art; avoid the Proustian bed" (p. 575). For Proust the personal past consists of discrete moments which can be resurrected in their wholeness. Calling up those moments into the present allows his Marcel to live, briefly, in the past and the present at once, and thus to escape from the prison of time:

> The truth surely was that the being within me which had enjoyed these impressions had enjoyed them because they had in

them something that was common to a day long past and to now, because in some way they were extra-temporal, and this being made its appearance only when, through one of these identifications of the present with the past, it was likely to find itself in the one and only medium in which it could exist and enjoy the essence of things, that is to say: outside time. This explained why it was that my anxiety on the subject of my death had ceased at the moment when I had unconsciously recognized the taste of the little madeleine, since the being which at that moment I had been was an extra-temporal being and therefore unalarmed by the vicissitudes of the future. This being had only come to me, only manifested itself outside of activity and immediate enjoyment, on those rare occasions when the miracle of an analogy had made me escape from the present. And only this being had the power to perform that task which had always defeated the efforts of my memory and my intellect, the power to make me rediscover days that were long past, the Time that was Lost.[5]

The differences between Marcel's description and Van's are important. First, Van's perception of the conjunction of past and present, rather than giving him a sense of liberation from time, makes him even more acutely aware of its immediate impingement. Second, and more important, Van's moment of perception confirms his belief that "nowness is the only reality we know" (p. 585). Past and present are not, in his understanding of time, the discrete realities they are for Proust; the past takes its meaning from its conjunction with the present, and it changes as the conditions of the present moment change.

In *Ada* as elsewhere in Nabokov's fiction, the past is never a pure, inviolable thing which can be resurrected intact. The shape and meaning of experience begin to be altered by memory and imagination the moment it becomes *past* experience—just as Van and Ada continue to revise and reshape the written record of their past as long as they live. The cumulative growth of the book in which Van records his past is, in fact, a close approximation of, even a metaphor for, the way the past itself grows and changes each time it is recollected in the present. Van makes this specific association himself, comparing the *Ada* we are reading to the Ada he recalls, in a passage in which he recounts attempting a mental experiment to "exercise the 'muscles of consciousness'—namely putting oneself back not merely into the frame of mind that had preceded a radical change in one's life, but into a state of complete ignorance regarding that change. He knew it could not be done, that not the achievement, but the obstinate attempt was possible, because he would not have remembered the preface to Ada had not life turned the next page, causing now its radiant text to flash through all the tenses of the mind" (pp. 500–501). Van's lived past, like his memoir, will take its final, finished shape only when both he and Ada are dead.

Van first decides to write his memoirs in 1892, when he and Ada are still hiding their incest from Demon and Marina, who are in turn hiding (less successfully) from the two young "cousins" the fact of their common parentage. The idea comes to Van when Ada shows him the album of compromising photographs taken by the prying kitchen boy, Kim, which Kim is now using to blackmail Ada. The album is a photographic record of life at Ardis Hall in the summer of 1884, with special emphasis on the furtive lovemaking of Van and Ada. Van is incensed, not so much at the treachery of Kim as at the treachery of the photographs themselves, which have "vulgarized our mind-pictures" (p. 430) of that erotically edenic summer. Van makes an angry resolution: "I will either horsewhip his eyes out or redeem our childhood by making a book of it: *Ardis*, a family chronicle" (p. 430). Unfortunately, Van chooses the first alternative as the most immediately rewarding, and it is not until sixty-four years later that the idea of writing his memoirs occurs to him again. By this time Demon and Marina are dead, there is no blackmailer and nothing to redeem, and the past has stretched out to include a great deal more than the summers of childhood. The motive on this occasion arises from Van's recognition that all his previous scientific and philosophical books have been, au fond, "buoyant and bellicose exercises in literary style"; all his philosophy, all his efforts to articulate the results of his researches, reduce to "a match between inspiration and design" (p. 614). He settles on the memoir as the genre which promises the grandest match, the most challenging exercise in literary style—a more pacific, though more difficult, alternative to satisfying inspiration by horsewhipping a man's eyes out. In Van's memoir, inspiration and design (or *Information and Form*, the title of a book written jointly by Van and Ada) translate into memory and language, and style becomes the measure of the extent to which memory and language give life, intensity, and meaning to each other.

To recall, Van discovers, is to create; the man is the father of the child he remembers. For this reason Van insists that the book's final section, which he begins writing on his ninety-seventh birthday, "is not meant as an epilogue; it is the true introduction of my ninety-seven percent true, and three percent likely, *Ada or Ardor, a family chronicle*" (p. 603). As old Van and Ada are the "flat pale parents of the future babes" (p. 625)—their young selves, still gestating in memory—so the true beginning of the book is in its end, in the picture of bedridden Van and Ada tirelessly reworking the manuscript as if it were a matter of life and death. As, of course, it is. They create themselves in creating the book, and when they die they, being themselves matters of style, die into the book, so that the family tree has no death dates for either of them.

Nabokov once commented that "the past is a constant accumulation of images, but our brain is not an ideal organ for constant retrospection and the best we can do is to pick out and try to retain those patches of rainbow light flitting through memory. The act of retention is the act of art, artistic selection, artistic blending, artistic re-combination of actual events" (*Strong Opinions*, p. 186). The Ada whom Van celebrates in his book, whom he loves more than his life, is herself a composite of remembered impressions, a creature who does not really exist outside of his imagination. Van can even recall the moment at which that composite image was formed, as he left Ardis at the end of his second summer there in a fit of jealous anger:

He could swear he did not look back, could not—by any optical chance, or in any prism—have seen her physically as he walked away; and yet, with dreadful distinction, he retained forever a composite picture of her standing where he left her. The picture—which penetrated him, through an eye in the back of his head, through his vitreous spinal canal, and could never be lived down, never—consisted of a selection and blend

of such random images and expressions of hers that had affected him with a pang of intolerable remorse at various moments in the past. . . .
Those were the fragments of the tesselation, and there were others, even more trivial; but in coming together the harmless parts made a lethal entity, and the girl in yellow slacks and black jacket, standing with her hands behind her back, slightly rocking her shoulders, leaning her back now closer now less closely against the tree trunk, and tossing her hair—a definite picture that he knew he had never seen in reality—remained within him more real than any actual memory. [Pp. 314–15]

Van creates Ada in much the same way that Humbert Humbert creates his Lolita. *That* pale fatal girl, however, is a slightly altered image of another child, Dolores Haze, and Humbert recognizes that his mistake was in adoring the first girl and ignoring the second. There is, on the other hand, no second Ada, no ordinary child waiting behind the image of the gitanilla to rebuke Van for his obsession. The difference is that Humbert pursues his vision across the recognizable landscape of America, and Van pursues his across the almost recognizable landscape of Antiterra. Had Humbert been a Demonian, an inhabitant of Antiterra (hindsight suggests that Humbert *is* a Demonian, though a misplaced one), he might well have lived contentedly past his ninety-seventh year with his Lolita. Antiterra is a fractured, dream-distorted, not quite symmetrical mirror image of our own planet, an imagined, "as-if" green world in which "artists are the only gods" (p. 553). It is an artist's image, created out of the commonplaces of terrestrial reality in the same way that Charles Kinbote's Zembla is created out of New Wye, though Antiterra has the autonomy that Kinbote tries unsuccessfully to give his Zembla. The autonomous, "scientifically ungraspable" (p. 20) reality of this imagined world is, like Van's image of Ada, a composite picture pieced together out of recognizable details.
Van's long description of his mental picture of Ada provides a gloss on Nabokov's attitude toward the way in which strong visual images are created—by the artist, or the lover, or anyone who attempts to recall a vivid impression. There is another, related gloss, this time on the proper response of the audience to

the kind of liberties the artist may take in creating his images. This passage appears in Demon Veen's description of the paintings of Hieronymous Bosch, one of which includes (Demon learns from Ada) a Tortoiseshell butterfly whose folded wings incorrectly display the patternings of the upper wing surface rather than the underside:

"If I could write," mused Demon, "I would describe, in too many words no doubt, how passionately, how incandescently, how incestuously—*c'est le mot*—art and science meet in an insect, in a thrush, in a thistle of that ducal bosquet. . . . I mean I don't give a hoot for the esoteric meaning, for the myth behind the moth, for the masterpiece-baiter who makes Bosch express some bosh of his time, I'm allergic to allegory and am quite sure he was just enjoying himself by crossbreeding casual fancies just for the fun of the contour and color, and what we have to study . . . is the joy of the eye, the feel and the taste of the woman-sized strawberry that you embrace *with* him, or the exquisite surprise of an unusual orifice." [Pp. 462–63]

Ada's fancies are crossbred carefully rather than casually, but the result is the same: in the novel, as in Bosch's paintings, the artist fractures familiar images and so jostles us out of our habitual responses, thus making us vulnerable to the shockingly unfamiliar sensation that, for a moment, we are participating in someone else's impressions.

In one of the few passages in the memoir which is identifiably hers ("Go on from here, Ada, please!" Van writes), Ada, the entomologist-botanist-actress-painter, instructs Van, the psychologist-philosopher-writer, in what is and must be the common objective of what Van later calls "the most exact arts and the wildest flights of pure science" (p. 232). Both artist and scientist, Ada says, are observers of the uncommon, of the "unprecedented and unrepeatable," of unnatural rather than natural history:

Unnatural history—because that precision of senses and sense must seem unpleasantly peculiar to peasants, and because the detail is all: The song of a Tuscan Firecrest or a Sitka King-

let in a cemetery cypress; a minty whiff of Summer Savory or
Yerba Buena on a coastal slope; the dancing flitter of a Holly
Blue or an Echo Azure—combined with other birds, flowers
and butterflies: *that* has to be heard, smelled and seen through
the transparency of death and ardent beauty. And the most
difficult: beauty itself as perceived through the there and then.
[P. 77]

We recognize in Ada's description of unnatural history a version
of one of the most fundamental of Nabokov's aesthetic premises.
Her progression from a single sensory detail to a combination of
details to "beauty itself" is reminiscent of Adam Krug's celebration of the word-image-pattern correlations in Shakespeare and
of John Shade's "combinational delight." Art—worthwhile, in-
sincere, inhuman, Nabokovian art—and pure science—lepi-
doptery, for example—both begin with the precise detail and
end with an autonomous, aesthetically satisfying, and therefore
intensely meaningful, pattern of details.

Nabokov's insistence that genius, artistic or otherwise, is a
matter of eccentric preoccupation with the "unnatural" and the
extraordinary lies behind his condescending treatment of Freud-
ians, careless translators, and all paraphrasts, careful or careless. His frontal attacks on these generalizers, especially the
paraphrasts, account for much of the humor in *Ada*. But paraphrase is a very different thing from parody, and the distinction
between the two is a crucial one in *Ada*. The narrative structure
of *Ada* is a parodistic mélange of traditional novelistic devices, a
kind of burlesque history of the evolution of the form.[6] To parody form is one thing, but to paraphrase (or mistranslate) a text
is quite another, as Van and Ada themselves insist. "Old storytelling devices," Van says, "may be parodied only by very great
and inhuman artists, but only close relatives can be forgiven for
paraphrasing illustrious poems." Ada agrees: "A paraphrase,
even my paraphrase, is like the corruption of 'snakeroot' into
'snagrel'—all that remains of a delicate little birthwort" (p. 260).

Narrative structures serve the very important purpose of giving art the formal, patterned, intentional shape that distinguishes it from untransformed experience. When Van and Ada
begin a series of clandestine meetings in Van's hotel room at

Mount Roux, Van comments that "the alberghian atmosphere of those new trysts added a novelistic touch (Aleksey and Anna may have asterisked here!) which Ada welcomed as a frame, as a form, something supporting and guarding life" (p. 553). Van's observation is an acknowledgment of the vital function of narrative structure as a means of imposing form. Van's parodies of narrative structure, on the other hand, suggest that the particular kind of narrative method the writer uses is a more or less arbitrary choice. He can parody these old storytelling devices and shift from one to the other at will just because they *are* devices. They are frames, supporting and guarding what is inviolable and unalterable in the work—the tesselated pattern of its images.

Nabokov's reductive attitude toward the function of narrative structure is an instance of the kind of willful perversity that is characteristic of his fiction. As *Ada* demonstrates, however, if the perversity is willful it is no more wanton than is Van's habit of walking on his hands. Van delights in his acrobatic perversity not because it proves the extent of his prowess, or because it disgusts some adults, amuses some, and frightens children, but simply because he likes the view. If one cannot turn the world upside down to see how it looks that way, one can at least turn himself upside down and have a look. In attempting to analyze the pleasure his "maniambulation" gave him, Van, writing about it more than sixty years later, concludes that the rapture of overcoming gravity was very much like the rapture of artistic revelation: "It was the standing of a metaphor on its head not for the sake of the trick's difficulty, but in order to perceive an ascending waterfall or a sunrise in reverse: a triumph, in a sense, over the ardis of time" (p. 197).

Van's memoir, *Ada*, is itself an extended simile stood on its head. The simile compares the two "unachieved, perhaps unachievable tasks" (p. 501) that obsess Van throughout the first half of his life: the task of knowing and possessing Ada completely, and the task of knowing and possessing the essence of time. Characteristically, it is Ada who actually sets up the figure of speech. She does so in a retort to Van who has been explaining to her his "Texture of Time" essay, a philosophical inquiry into the nature of time. " 'I wonder,' said Ada, "I wonder if the attempt to discover those things is worth the stained glass. We can know the time, we can know a time. We can never know Time. Our senses are simply not meant to perceive it. It is like—'" (p. 599). Ada's unfinished sentence comes at the end of part 4, just before the final section, which was added after the first draft was completed and which Van describes as the proper prologue to the whole. The early chapters of the book examine in fine detail the part of the simile that Ada leaves unstated: attempting to know time as a palpable, perceptual thing is like trying to know and possess fully another human being.

What disturbs the young Van is his sense of limitation, of being able to know time only as memory, to know other people only as reminders of themselves or of someone or something else (Lucette reminds Van of Ada; Ada reminds Lucette of Van; Aqua reminds Demon of Marina; Marina reminds Demon of a Parmiagnino painting—and so on), to know the complex structure of the created world only as a perplexing riddle whose answer is everywhere hinted at but never revealed. "The strength, the dignity, the delight of man," eighteen-year-old Van says, "is to spite and despise the shadows and stars that hide their secrets from us" (p. 32). Fifty-two-year-old Van has begun to see that Ada is right: both the tasks he sets himself are finally unachievable. Van's essay acknowledges that for even the most ardent lover of time "three or four seconds of what can be felt as nowness . . . is the only reality we know" (p. 585). The rest of time—that is, the past, since Van rejects any notion of future time—is knowable only as a gappy accumulation of sensory impressions. Similarly, in analyzing his erotic obsession with Ada, Van recognizes that only at the height of their lovemaking did he really know her; only then did reality lose "the quotes it wore like claws. . . . For one spasm or two, he was safe" (p. 232). But just as the present moment is actually only the visible edge of the past, as Van concludes in his essay, so that contact with naked reality in moments of ardent physical intensity "always was and is a form of memory, even at the moment of perception" (p. 233).

From their first Ardis summer on, Ada's tendency to be soberly systematic and objective balances, and sometimes undercuts, Van's sensuality, emotiveness, and subjectivity. Ada, for example, can distinguish among the varieties of fireflies that visit Ardis and knows their Latin names. Van's reaction to the fireflies is of another order altogether:

Van watched them with the same pleasurable awe he had experienced as a child, when, lost in the purple crepuscule of an Italian hotel garden, in an alley of cypresses, he supposed they were golden ghouls or the passing fancies of the garden. . . . The presence of those magnificent little animals delicately illuminating, as they passed, the fragrant night, filled Van with a subtle exhilaration that Ada's entomology seldom evoked in him—maybe in result of the abstract scholar's envy which a naturalist's immediate knowledge sometimes provokes. [P. 78]

Van muses about the nature of time and space, while Ada turns light and moving shadows—time measured by space—into the counters of a game with strict rules and a rigid scoring system. Ada is good at Scrabble; Van is better at chess. It is only logical, then, that Ada, the physical scientist and realist who very early impresses Van and the reader with the "pictorial and architectural details of her metaphysics" (p. 81), should provide the metaphor that allows Van, the philosopher, to translate his fuzzy speculations into the concrete details of a love story.

But *Ada* is not only Van's memoir; it is also Nabokov's novel, and the story of the transformation of the incestuous lovers Van and Ada into Vaniada is in turn *his* metaphor for the collapsing of a metaphor into a comprehensive vision of a multifaceted world (or an *Ambidextrous Universe*, to borrow another title from *Ada*, this one identifiable from its context as an allusion to *Pale Fire*).[7] The objective and subjective, the tenor and the vehicle of the metaphor, require each other. A metaphor, as Van explains in a digression on the fallacies of Freudian dream interpretation, compares "two real, concrete, existing things. . . . Neither is a symbol of the other," even if the comparison is between a "real experience" and a "real commonplace object"—between an inner and an outer reality (p. 385). The two parts of the metaphor can, however, have only a family resemblance. Lucette sitting on Van's lap reminds him of Ada sitting there four years earlier: "Family smell; yes, coincidence: a set of coincidences slightly displaced; the artistry of asymmetry" (p. 296). To perceive and marvel at those asymmetrical coincidences between the inner reality and the outer is the province of memory and art: that kind of vision, which requires "*third sight* (individual, magically detailed imagination)" (p. 266), can be sustained only on Antiterra, an imagined world where artists are the only gods.

This Demonian setting of Antiterra allows Nabokov the freedom to construct a world out of bits and pieces of other imagined, literary worlds and to invent for his characters a way of speaking that indicates just how thoroughly comfortable they are in a world made up entirely of words. The reader of *Ada*, however, who is likely to consider language an arbitrary means of communication and not part of a necessary way of being, can find Antiterra a place of difficult access. *Ada* is a paranomastic playground, full of bilingual and trilingual puns, verbal puzzles, and allusions to the literature of three languages. The resulting density and difficulty of the text can seem an insurmountable and unnecessary barrier to the reader, even to one who has worked his way to *Ada* through the complexities of the other novels. The problem is not, of course, unique to Nabokov: Joyce, Eliot, and Pound, for example, present similar problems for their readers, and their work has occasioned similar disagreements about whether in being difficult to read a writer is being inventive and ingenious or precious and perverse. I believe the most intellectually honest answer to such questions is the one George Steiner gives in discussing the complexity of *Ada*: "In the main," Steiner says, "this kind of disagreement is a matter of olives: one has the taste or one doesn't."[8] Still, difficult writers are all difficult in their own ways, and there are things that can be said about the particular kinds of problems Nabokov's fiction poses for the reader, and about the reasons for their presence.

In the first place, the allusions and word play in Nabokov's novels are reminders of the distinctions that must be made between the ideal, abstract world of art, where problems are susceptible of elegant solutions, and the real mutable world of actual experience, where they usually are not. Elegant solutions are also possible in games like chess, and what the novels have to say about art is that its appeal is that of a splendidly complex, inventive game, and the pleasure it affords is the aesthetic pleasure of solving a difficult puzzle or discovering, in Nabokov's words, "something in a scrambled picture—Find What the Sailor Has Hidden—that the finder cannot unsee once it has been seen" (*Speak, Memory*, p. 229). As Van Veen says of one of his own discoveries, "How meager! How magic!" (p. 586).

Word play and allusion have a more specific function in these novels as well. Puns, anagrams, homonyms, and look-alike words are all evidence of the fragility of language—especially written language—and the tenuousness of its hold on meaning. The novel which most explicitly examines that relationship is *Transparent Things*, but we have seen in *Pale Fire* that the accidental substitution of one letter for another in a printed word was sufficient to revolutionize John Shade's thinking about life and death. It is appropriate that Van and Ada enjoy playing Scrabble, a game in which the counters are letters and the pattern of play is determined by the chance alignment of words. It is even more appropriate that the set they play with was given to them by one Baron Klim Avidov—an anagrammatically disguised Vladimir Nabokov, for whom the game of words that is a novel holds the same kind of fascination as the grander game of worlds it imitates.

Ada, the most allusive of the novels, also provides the best example of the way Nabokov's allusions work. At times it appears that Nabokov has taken a page from his own book on Gogol and introduced the kind of "charming" allusion that originates in sheer playfulness and goes nowhere—such as the translation of Baudelaire's name into "Goodgrief" (*beau douleur*) or the collapsing of Eugene O'Neill and Thomas Mann into "one Eelmann," author of *Love under the Lindens*. More often, the allusions work to enrich the texture of the novel (and complicate it in the process) and to broaden the implications of its themes. The two best examples in *Ada* are the mismatched pair of writers alluded to most often in the novel, Chateaubriand and Tolstoy. Part of the reason for the presence of Chateaubriand is easy enough to see, since he created probably the most famous pair of romantic siblings in world literature. In addition, his René was also a victim of a strain of the same insatiable itch that plagues Van and Ada; hence Chateaubriand's mosquito, the virulent insect that swarms through Ardis every summer attacking those with tender skin— especially Ada—and leaving them to suffer the fire of the bite and indulge the exquisite pleasure of scratching.[9] There is another and more complicated reason for the allusions to Chateaubriand. We know of his passionate childhood attachment to his own sister Lucile, and of his grief at her early death. It is not coincidental that the Lucette of *Ada* is also called Lucile, or that Van (whom Ada at times calls René) does not feel the same passion for her that he feels for Ada, and will not indulge the attraction he does feel. The incest that interests Nabokov is in Chateaubriand's fiction, not in his biography; he introduces the suggestion of the biographical parallel, with its potential psychological implications, only to reject it in favor of the iconographical richness of the fictional parallel.

The appropriateness of the many allusions to Tolstoy's *Anna Karenina* are equally clear. It is also a family chronicle which juxtaposes two kinds of love—the possessive sensuality of Eros and the spirituality and selflessness of Anteros. Ada and Van share initials with Anna and Vronsky, another couple who defy family and social convention for the sake of their love. Tolstoy's defiant lovers come to a bad end, of course, while the more gentle, conventional, and spiritually sensitive Levin and Kitty live happily ever after. Characteristically, Nabokov improves on Tolstoy's moral polarities by arranging a merger: his Van and Ada live *contentedly* ever after somewhere between heaven and hell, nurturing their healthy, faithful love into old age with good doses of purely physical lust—sometimes for each other and sometimes not.

The problems that the word play and allusion in Nabokov's novels create for the reader, then, are part of a necessary trade-off for the richness and complexity they contribute. But I think we still have not fully answered the question; that is, I think we can go on to speculate that another reason for the difficulty of the novels is traceable to a form of authorial arrogance, that his complex style was for Nabokov at once a way of distancing himself from his books and of putting the books out of the reach of the wrong kinds of readers. Nabokov was insistent, obsessively so, that a writer's private life was not to be found in his books, and he warned his readers that they would be misguided if the similarities they might see between himself and his characters should ever lead them to "say 'aha' and identify the designer with the design" (*The Gift*, p. i). Van Veen also wrote a novel in which he attempted to keep his characters and situations at a distance from his own emotional life, but failed because he had not yet developed a style that could function as a successful buffer. When each of his three female characters begins, to Van's dismay, to resemble dark-haired, intelligent Ada, all that Van can do is to transform each of them into a "bromidic dummy with a dun bun" (p. 361).[10] Another of Nabokov's novelists, Sebastian Knight, succeeds where Van fails: the sly poses of his novels, and the intricate games they play, protect Sebastian from the prying of the Mr. Goodmans of the world, those critics who insist on extrapolating from the work to the life.

Nietzsche says that "all the more subtle laws of any style have their origin at this point: they at the same time keep away, create a distance, forbid 'entrance' . . . while they open the ears of those whose ears are related to ours."[11] Sebastian's style succeeds in protecting his books by keeping their caviar out of the hands of the general, fending off readers like the businessman who gave up after reading one or two because "he preferred books that made one think, and Knight's books didn't,—they left you puzzled and cross" (*Knight*, p. 181). I suspect that Nabokov intended for his style to provide the same sort of protection that Sebastian Knight's did, to be a way of hiding the Grail (to paraphrase Robert Frost) and putting a spell on it so the wrong ones, the ones who can't be saved anyway, won't find it. The novels impose their own process of natural selection, weeding out the kind of readers who flourish in the Padukgrad of *Bend Sinister*, the kind who delight in a vapid comic strip about the domestic trials of a very dull Everyman or who read *Hamlet* as political propaganda. Nabokov did not conceal his intense dislike, and distrust, of readers who were not sufficiently awestruck by the sheer artistic genius of works which he admired, and who were interested only in what those works had to say about the person who wrote them or about the time and place in which they were written. Here, for example, is his comment on the treatment of Pushkin's *Eugene Onegin* in Russian criticism— complete with a Parthian shot apparently aimed at his own detractors:

Thus a character borrowed from books but brilliantly recomposed by a great poet to whom life and library were one, placed by that poet within a brilliantly reconstructed environment, and played with by that poet in a succession of compositional patterns—lyrical impersonations, tomfooleries of genius, literary parodies, and so on—is treated by Russian pedants as a sociological and historical phenomenon typical of Alexander I's regime (alas, this tendency to generalize and vulgarize the unique fancy of an individual genius has also its advocates in the United States). [*Eugene Onegin*, 2:151]

"Generalize" and "vulgarize" are the key words—the arrogant words—in this passage. (Nabokov despised Freud precisely because he saw in the "Viennese quack" the tendency to generalize and vulgarize the fascinating eccentricities of human behavior.) A playful and difficult style was for Nabokov one way of protecting the unique fancy of *his* individual genius from an audience of levelers and idea men.

Nabokov's own first audience was his mother, to whom he read the elegy he composed at the age of fifteen, and after his marriage almost all of his books were dedicated to his wife, Vera. While I think it would be a waste of energy to speculate about the psychological influence these two women may have had on Nabokov's art, they do share the characteristics of the ideal audience of gentle readers for a Nabokov novel—an audience that is intelligent, well read, multilingual, understanding of Nabokov's strong attachment to his old-world past, and, most important, sympathetic from the outset. Such an audience would not only know where to look for the Grail but would recognize it as a holy object when they found it.

It is interesting to note that most of Nabokov's fictional writers in the English novels (Mr. R. of *Transparent Things* is the one exception among the major characters) are willing to trust their unfinished manuscripts to only one reader, and in each case that reader is the woman who shares the writer's private life. Sebastian Knight will allow only Clare Bishop to see his novels before they are finished; John Shade reads *Pale Fire* section by section to his wife, Sybil—much to the consternation of Charles Kinbote; Ada Veen lies in bed with Van, reading, commenting on, and occasionally adding to his manuscript; and Vadim Vadimovich of *Look at the Harlequins!* goes through three failed marriages before he finds the woman he has needed all along, the only one of the four who understands and appreciates his work. The scenes in which we see these writers sharing their work with the women are usually set in very circumscribed, domestic, even intimate places—a bedroom or a lighted kitchen at night— where the writer and his work are protected from the prowling Kinbotes outside. All these women are literate, intelligent, and lovingly sympathetic. The essential function they serve is best suggested by Vadim Vadimovich's musings as he mentally follows his lover-confidante's progress through his manuscript:

I could say what I do not remember having been moved to say in years, namely: My happiness was complete. As I walked, I read those cards with you, at your pace, your diaphanous index at my rough peeling temple, my wrinkled finger at your turquoise temple-vein. . . . You knew my work too well to be ruffled by a too robust erotic detail, or annoyed by a too recondite literary allusion. It was bliss reading *Ardis* with you that way. . . . Was I an excellent writer? I was an excellent writer. [*Harlequins*, pp. 232–34]

The writer, no matter how private his work may be, needs a receptive audience that he can write for; and as a vulnerable human being, he needs assurance that his work is worth doing and that he does it well. The intelligent, sympathetic woman can answer both these needs, and for Sebastian Knight, John Shade, Van Veen, Vadim Vadimovich N., and, I suspect, for Vladimir Vladimirovich Nabokov, that woman was both the one critic he could fully trust and the one audience whose opinion finally mattered.

Seven

Transparent Things

Ada, published in 1969, was followed three years later by a book that seems designed to be all that *Ada* is not. While *Ada* is the longest and most allusive of Nabokov's novels, *Transparent Things* is the shortest and least allusive; Van Veen's comprehensive memoir, which is chronologically arranged, begins before Van's birth and follows him through his ninety-seven or more years. The span covered by *Transparent Things* is a single moment of arrested time, an instant of *temps meublé* filled up with the narrator's randomly digressive forays into the antecedents of that moment. The first book ends with a narrative maneuver that allows the two major characters to avoid the obligatory death scene, while the second ends with the major character's death. The protagonists of the two books, Van Veen and Hugh Person, are polar opposites in nearly every respect. Van is a professional writer, a self-confident intellectual with awesome athletic and sexual prowess, who is loved to distraction by several women; Hugh Person is a professional reader, sexually and athletically inept, and an object of contempt to the one woman he loves. Perhaps the most emphatic difference between the two books is the difference in tone. Van's ironic voice frequently slips into unguarded, naked sentimentality, especially when he describes his need for Ada, his various partings with her, and their mutual grief at Lucette's suicide. The narrator of *Transparent Things*, on the other hand, remains consistently clinical and dispassionate, even when his characters suffer in love or death.

Nabokov's strong resistance to being typed as a writer or to being too closely identified with any of his characters, especially his narrators, might be a sufficient, if not particularly satisfying, explanation for his writing a book that is in so many blatant ways the opposite of its immediate predecessor. But even if that kind of deliberate perversity was a factor in the design of *Transparent Things*, it does not preclude other, less speculative reasons for the differences, reasons that have to do with the opposing thematic concerns of each book. By over-generalizing, it is possible to see *Ada* as an extended, metaphoric exploration of the *ars longa, vita brevis* cliché—an assessment of what it means to say not only that art tells enduring truths, but even that art is triumphant over death. *Transparent Things* then appends two caveats to *Ada*. In the first place, it makes a case for the fragility of all our metaphors, and thus of all our art; if we look to the words of art for the large truths by which our private worlds are oriented, then we must be prepared for a slip of the tongue or pen to reverse the poles or set the earth spinning in the opposite direction. Second, *Transparent Things* demonstrates that there is a catch-22 problem inherent in the whole notion that art, because its internal laws are aesthetic, can circumvent the laws of biological necessity; the problem is simply that our fictions may require death as an *aesthetic* necessity—a way of closing that is finally a matter of style.

All of Nabokov's major characters in the novels prior to *Transparent Things* take time out at some point to speculate about the meaning of death and the nature of the hereafter. None of them, however, is able to arrive at anything more than a cautious, qualified answer to his own questions. V in *Sebastian Knight* concludes that "the hereafter may be the full ability of consciously living in any chosen soul"; Pnin believes "dimly" that "the souls of the dead, perhaps, formed committees, and these, in continuous session, attended to the destinies of the quick"; Humbert Humbert is finally reconciled to the cold comfort of seeing the "refuge of art" as "the only immortality you and I may share," but his careful wording leaves other possibilities open; John Shade is "reasonably sure that we survive"—but Shade, who died on July 21, was also "reasonably sure" that he would be alive on July 22.[1] The three characters who never are able to arrive at even a tentative resolution of the question are the three who are saved from death by an egregious manipulation of the narrative. The narrator of *Bend Sinister* feels enough pity for Adam Krug in his panic at approaching death to spare him, first by granting him a saving madness, then by simply ending the novel and declaring that Krug, as a fictional character, never had to die anyway. Van and Ada Veen, characteristically, cannot agree on what the other world is like or even whether there is one. Ada contends that anyone is free to imagine whatever version of immortality he chooses; Van counters that logic always intervenes to destroy the happy illusion. Van and Ada, like Krug, needn't have worried about the other world, because they never have to leave their own. The end of their book brings them full circle, back to the nursery at Ardis where they began. They too are saved by a stylistic miracle. Immortality is, for them, only a matter of the mental rearrangement of chapters.

The one Nabokov character who can speak with authority about the afterlife is the narrator of *Transparent Things*. This narrator, a successful novelist identified only as Mr. R., knows whereof he speaks, since, as we learn in the course of his narrative, he died a painful death from cancer in a hospital in Bologna. *Transparent Things* is his commentary, issued from beyond the grave, on the life and death of one Hugh Person, a very unremarkable young editor with Mr. R.'s publishing firm. But Mr. R. is not willing to divulge all that he knows, either about where he is or what he now understands about mortal life or its sequel. He teases us by declaring that, given his new perspective, "there are no mysteries now," but to reveal some secrets "would entail explications and revelations too sad, too frightful to face" (p. 22). Mr. R. is a literally omniscient narrator, whose pontifical tone is a constant reminder that he knows far more about what is going on here than do either the people in his account or the readers of it.

I say the *people* in his account, not the characters, because R. is the only one of Nabokov's narrators who does not try to turn his story into a work of art—a novel, or, as Kinbote puts it, the monstrous semblance of a novel—by imposing on it the artificial shapeliness of a plot. His commentary is not an attempt to recast the past in more comprehensible or more acceptable terms, or to give it the durability of imaginative art. Instead, it is simply an effort to explain why the progress of an ordinary human life is so fascinating to a detached and disinterested, inhuman, omniscient observer. This narrator announces his presence and his intentions frequently enough to alert us that his narrative is not intended to be a novel, but a kind of instructive or illustrative report: "Here's the person I want. Hullo, person!" (p. 1); "More in a moment" (p. 2); "Let us now illustrate our difficulties" (p. 5); "we must complete our report" (p. 32); "We shall close the subject on this bizarre note" (p. 93); "Let us make this a little clearer" (p. 94).

Still, *Transparent Things* is finally a novel, as its title page announces, and the author whose name appears there is not Mr. R. but Vladimir Nabokov. That author has a personal interest in Mr. R.'s report for several reasons. In the first place, he appears anagramatically as Adam von Librikov in R.'s *Tralatitions*, a novel which R. admits is a roman à clef with various of his contemporaries hidden away in the niches of his text. R. seems to know the people he parodies, including the original of von Librikov, well enough not to worry about their reactions to finding themselves in his book: "the customers whom he was accused of portraying were much too cool to announce their presence and their resentment. In fact they would rather enjoy listening to the tattle in literary salons with a little knowing air, as the French say" (p. 70). And, in keeping with the tangled small-world coincidences of *Transparent Things*, we learn that Hugh Person probably knows this same cool customer. Hugh's third trip to Europe is made, "at his firm's request, to look up Mr. R. and another American writer, also residing in Switzerland" (p. 68). Hullo, Mr. Nabokov.

The normally rigid distinctions among the collaborators who participate in bringing a book to life—writer, editor, reader, and character—have thus been broken down, and some unusual alliances formed. Vladimir Nabokov is at once the author of *Transparent Things*, an incidental character in it, and presumably a reader of Mr. R.'s *Tralatitions*; Mr. R. is the source of the story of *Transparent Things*, a character in it, and presumably a reader of Nabokov, whom he caricatures in his novel; Hugh Person is the editor of *Tralatitions*, a character in *Transparent Things*, and, as

"you, person" (his wife pronounces his name "you"), the anonymous reader of it. Mr. R. forms a unilateral alliance with Hugh,
who is for him "the person I want" for the purposes of his report. The more important alliance, however, is between R. and
Nabokov. R.'s use of the authorial *we* seems at first to be only a
narrative convention, but as the book progresses it gradually becomes clear that his plural pronoun has a definite referent, that
he is speaking for certain other like-minded people who are interested, as R. is, in the mechanics of storytelling and story writing. (D. Barton Johnson has pointed out that the English letter
R, when reversed, is the Cyrillic equivalent of the pronoun *I*.[2] In
addition, R.'s abbreviated name shades phonetically into *our* as
easily as Hugh's shades into *you*.) When he describes Hugh Person rereading an edited manuscript, R. observes that "through
the translucidity of the textual flow he was still correcting proof
as some of us try to do—mending a broken letter here, indicating italics there" (p. 75). Later he comments that "we depend on
italics to an even greater degree than do, in their arch quaint-
ness, writers of children's books" (p. 92), and again that "we
have shown our need for quotation marks" (p. 93). One of that
shadowy "we" group of superior observers is Nabokov, standing outside the book and watching his characters, first Mr. R.
and then Hugh Person, climb out of their fictional world by
means of what R. calls "the mysterious mental maneuver
needed to pass from one state of being to another" (p. 104). R.,
having died first, is there to assist Hugh in making his difficult
maneuver, and in fact his entire account is a moment's vision,
registered as he helps Hugh over the threshold. The opening
and closing lines of the book—addressed to Hugh, whose death
in a hotel fire is described in the final paragraph—are continuous: "Here's the person I want. Hullo, person! Doesn't hear me.
. . . Easy, you know, does it, son" (pp. 1, 104). What comes in
between is a commentary, in the form of a series of marginal annotations and emendations, on the last eighteen years of Hugh's
life.

   Mr. R.'s oracular utterances, we realize, are made from a diminished or highly restricted Elysium, one reserved for fictional
characters who escape from their circumscribed fictional world,
and his new omniscience is no more—though no less—than a

novelist's-eye view of a universe bounded by the covers of a book. As I suggested earlier, however, R. is not creating this world; that was done by Nabokov. He is simply reading its text carefully, in the same way that Hugh Person in his professional capacity as editor reads the proofs of R.'s own novels:

Hugh liked to read a set of proofs twice, once for the defects of the type and once for the virtues of the text. It worked better, he believed, if the eye check came first and the mind's pleasure next. He was now enjoying the latter and while not looking for errors, still had a chance to catch a missed boo-boo—his own or the printer's. . . . Hugh read with interest and concentration, but through the translucidity of the textual flow he still was correcting proof as some of us try to do—mending a broken letter here, indicating italics there, his eye and his spine (the true reader's main organ) collaborating rather than occluding each other. [Pp. 74–75]

Mr. R. also reads with a dual interest in text and typography, and he makes his marginal comments with the same emotional indifference as Hugh Person does. While he was alive—that is, while he participated as a character in the novel's story—R. exhibited a respectable range of normal human responses to various other characters: tender love for his stepdaughter Julia, hatred for his scheming secretary Tamworth, and sympathetic interest in the welfare of Hugh, "one of the nicest persons I knew" (p. 83). As a detached reader of the world as text, however, R. remains unmoved by anything that happens to the people in the book, even their deaths. For example, here is his description of the ignominious, trouserless death of Hugh Person's rather pathetic father, in the dressing room of a shabby clothing store:

Spatial disarrangement and dislocation have always their droll side, and few things are funnier than three pairs of trousers tangling in a frozen dance on the floor—brown slacks, blue jeans, old pants of gray flannel. Awkward Person Senior had been struggling to push a shod foot through the zigzag of a narrow trouser leg when he felt a roaring redness fill his head.

He died before reaching the floor, as if falling from some great height, and now lay on his back, one arm outstretched, umbrella and hat out of reach in the tall looking glass. [Pp. 14–15]

R. is interested only in the curious and amusing arrangement of tangled trousers on the floor, one of the patterns that are the virtues of a carefully planned text.

The striking difference between R.'s emotional involvement with the people he knows and his apparent indifference to the fates of the people he reads about deserves further comment, especially if we understand R. to be, in Nabokov's terms, the ideal reader who shares in the perspective of the artist whose book he is reading. Nabokov has consistently described himself as an "inhuman" artist and has just as consistently denounced "sincerity" in literature as a form of easy sentimentality—a case of a weak heart occluding both eye and spine. Not until *Transparent Things*, however, has he specifically confronted the charge, leveled at him by many readers, that he is coldly indifferent to the characters he creates, especially to their sufferings.[3] R. provides part of the answer to that charge by the change in his attitude; as a reader R. knows that fictive lives and fictive deaths are both matters of style, that people in books live and die only to help their creator shape the pattern that his particular vision requires. That fact, however, does not prevent the creator as man from feeling toward his creatures an attachment that he as artist cannot reveal, and this particular dilemma is addressed by Nabokov in *Transparent Things* in a characteristically oblique way. Hugh Person kills the only woman he has ever loved by strangling her while he is dreaming. Later in the novel the introduction of a minor character, an Englishman named Mr. Wilde who discourses on the laxity of the modern attitude toward crime, suggests that Nabokov intends to direct our attention to Oscar Wilde's dictum in "The Ballad of Reading Gaol" that "each man kills the thing he loves." The artist may well love certain of his people and still kill them, in the dream world of his fiction, as dispassionately as Hugh Person kills Armande in his dream. In both cases, the emotions and sympathies of the dreamer are subordinated to the aesthetic demands of the dream, which is an altogether different thing from diurnal life.[4]

R. at one point draws a specific analogy between dream fictions and literary fictions in describing Hugh's dreams, especially his erotic nightmares, which R. refers to as drafts and revisions of "the same, otherwise inexisting, story":

He desired to stress the following point with the fullest, fiercest, anti-Freudian force. Those oneiric torments had nothing to do, either directly or in a "symbolic" sense, with anything he had experienced in conscious life. The erotic theme was just one theme among others, as *A Boy for Pleasure* remained just an extrinsic whimsy in relation to the whole fiction of the serious, too serious writer who had been satirized in a recent novel.

In another no less ominous nocturnal experience, he would find himself trying to stop or divert a trickle of grain or fine gravel from a rift in the texture of space and being hampered in every conceivable respect by cobwebby, splintery, filamentary elements, confused heaps and hollows, brittle debris, collapsing colossuses. He was finally blocked by masses of rubbish, and *that* was death. Less frightening but perhaps imperiling a person's brain to an even greater extent were the "avalanche" nightmares at the rush of awakening when their imagery turned into the movement of verbal colluvia in the valleys of Toss and Thurn, whose gray rounded rocks, *Roches étonnées*, are so termed because of their puzzled and grinning surface, marked by dark "goggles" (*écarquillages*). Dream-man is an idiot not wholly devoid of animal cunning; the fatal flaw in his mind corresponds to the splutter produced by tongue twisters: "the risks scoundrels take." [Pp. 59–60]

The writer, according to R., shares the dreamer's problems: how to keep his fictions from being interpreted as symbolic or as condensations of the entirety of his conscious experience; how to keep his fantasy world whole and apart, without those tricklings from the "real" world that turn the dream into a nightmare; and how to create a world and hold it steadily in view without being swept away by the rush of his own words or enticed away by the temptation to follow his fascinating words in whatever direction their nuances of sound and sense may suggest. The writer's success depends in large part on the imperiousness of his control over the arrangement of the furnishings of his fictive world— and that must include his characters.

Throughout his commentary R. demonstrates his fascination —the true reader's fascination—with spatial and temporal arrangement in both the text and the type of this proof he is reading. R. speaks of events and people, rather than of plot and character, but the world he describes is still the world of a novel, and his commentary becomes a kind of *apologia* for the aesthetic premises of his friend and ally, Vladimir Nabokov. What R. says about time, hence about the structure of a plot, is first that "the future has no such reality (as the pictured past and the perceived present possess); the future is but a figure of speech, a specter of thought" (p. 1) and second that "every cause-and-effect sequence is always a hit-and-miss affair" (p. 92). If plot has a metaphoric—or tralatitious—function, if it is the imaginative equivalent of experiential reality, then it must be as faithful to the misses as it is to the hits. "The king died, and the queen died" is as valid a plot as "The king died, and then the queen died of grief." The first is, in fact, the better plot. It is not a *process* of causally related events which move toward a predetermined end, but an observed *pattern* of coincidental events that do not presuppose a causally determined future. Such a plot, indeed, takes no account of time as chronological progression or movement. The future does not exist, and the present is merely a prism through which to view the fragments of the past, now arranging themselves into patterns whose configurations are spatial, not temporal. From R.'s point of view, people and objects as they are found in the present are "transparent things, through which the past shines!" (p. 1).

The matters that R. attends to in his story of Hugh Person compose just such a plot. He notes the appearance of characters with the same or similar names; here and there the "muffled shock of an incomplete coincidence" (p. 11); the occurrence of dreams that, in retrospect, might be interpreted as prophetic; a shuttlecock landing on the same spot on the same sidewalk where one landed eight years before; the random crisscrossing of the destinies of the book's people.[5] These patterns of hits and near misses are the raison d'être of his story; there is no cause-

and-effect sequence, and the future reduces to a grammatical tense which, ironically, can be used only in speaking of what is already past. Hugh's death, which is the point at which R. begins and ends his report, is itself the result of a series of incomplete coincidences. Hugh kills his wife, whom he loves devotedly, in an act too volitionless to be called murder; he strangles her in the course of a dream in which he believes he is actually saving a young woman who leaps from the window of a burning building. Eight years later Hugh returns to the town where he first met his wife, and checks into the same hotel he had stayed in on that earlier visit. Someone, probably a disgruntled waiter who, we are told, had been fired after a fracas in the hotel dining room, chooses that night to set the hotel afire, and Hugh, awakened from a dream of his wife by the smell of smoke, perishes with the rest of the hotel guests. Another death, another interesting pattern of dislocated coincidences.

Mr. R. chooses Hugh as the subject of his commentary in part because as an editor Hugh is, like himself, interested in and alert to the vagaries of type on the printed page. We learn, for instance, that the only poem Hugh ever had published began with a witty demonstration of the relationship between meaning and the spatial arrangement of words on a page:

> Blest are suspension dots . . . The sun was setting
> a heavenly example to the lake . . . [P. 22]

On his first trip to Europe Hugh is amused by the arrangement of letters on a photo booth sign, which almost produces an Anglo-French pun:

$$3P\begin{matrix} \text{hotos} \\ \text{oses} \end{matrix}$$

[P. 14]

More important, both Hugh and R. are keenly aware of the fragility of a fictional world, which can be altered or destroyed by seemingly minor changes in the conventions that govern the appearance of type on a printed page.

R. remarks, shortly before the end of the book, that the proofreader's marks "with which Hugh Person still peppers the margins of galleys have a metaphysical or zodiacal import" (p. 93), and offers an illustrative example in defense of his remark:

Men have learned to live with a black burden, a huge aching hump: the supposition that "reality" may be only a "dream." How much more dreadful it would be if the very awareness of your being aware of reality's dreamlike nature were also a dream, a built-in hallucination! One should bear in mind, however, that there is no mirage without a vanishing point, just as there is no lake without a closed circle of reliable land.
    We have shown our need for quotation marks ("reality," "dream").

Hugh Person dies, and his book collapses around him, because his proofreader fails him at the last moment. There are no quotation marks to turn either reality or dream into a conceptualized notion; both are actual, both must be contended with, and Hugh becomes fatally confused. He has fallen asleep while waiting for the pretty desk clerk, with whom he has nervously made an assignation, to come to his room. As he drifts off to sleep, his imagination substitutes his dead wife Armande for the tempting stranger. "Person, *this* person," R. observes, "was on the imagined brink of imagined bliss when Armande's footfalls approached—striking out both 'imagined' in the proof's margin (never too wide for corrections and queries!)." (Mr. R. seems to have used this sentence as an object lesson in just how burdened printed words can be with conventions that must be used properly. Note the distinction between "Person" and "person," the italics, dash, comma, quotation marks, apostrophe, parentheses, and exclamation mark.) Hugh suddenly awakes from his dream of Armande, choking from the thick smoke that is filling his room. In his confusion he opens the door instead of the window, letting in even more of the lethal smoke. That mistake is fatal, and Hugh dies, still confused, still not knowing—as we do—that the state of being which he would call "reality" is actually only the dream of the artist who created him.

Crumbling partitions of plaster and wood allowed human cries to reach him, and one of his last wrong ideas was that those were the shouts of people anxious to help him, and not the howls of fellow men. Rings of blurred colors circled around him, reminding him briefly of a childhood picture in a frightening book about triumphant vegetables whirling faster and faster around a nightshirted boy trying desperately to awake from the iridescent dizziness of dream life. Its ultimate vision was the incandescence of a book or a box grown completely transparent and hollow. This is, I believe, *it*: not the crude anguish of physical death but the incomparable pangs of the mysterious mental maneuver needed to pass from one state of being to another. [P. 104]

Transparent Things, the record of a dream life, collapses with the walls of the burning room, and Hugh is now free to climb out of his fictional world and join those other two amateurs of the printed word who have taken such an interest in his case, Mr. R. and Mr. Nabokov. The real life of Hugh Person escapes; we know nothing of him during the large gaps of time that R. skips over so breezily, and little enough of what he thinks and feels at any given moment. Even a privileged narrator like R., who is able to penetrate what Nabokov once called "the web of when and where,"[6] cannot locate the living person in that web or capture him in the words of his report. What we are left with are the marginal comments, corrections, and queries that encircle the text of a fictive life.

Eight

Look at the Harlequins!

Nabokov's last novel, *Look at the Harlequins!*, is so strikingly similar to another carnival piece, Yeats's "The Circus Animals' Desertion," as to suggest that Nabokov may well have had the poem in mind when he wrote the novel. Both were written near the end of a long career, both rehearse old themes and reintroduce old characters, both suggest that, to use Yeats's terms, the "players and painted stage" of art are "emblems" of "heart-mysteries" that cannot be spoken, and that the complex human emotions that give rise to the "dream" of art are soon forgotten in the enchantment of the dream itself. Finally, both writers end by dismissing their familiar circus creatures and returning to what Yeats calls "the foul rag-and-bone shop of the heart" and Nabokov calls "Reality."[1] These similarities are interesting, but the differences between the two are more instructive. Yeats's poem is a reluctant acknowledgment of the need for a kind of abasement, for returning to a foul place where one must lie down before beginning to climb out again into the purer, cleaner atmosphere of art. Nabokov's novel, on the other hand, rejoices in rather than laments that same return; the "raving slut" of Yeats's poem is replaced in Nabokov's book by "my ultimate and immortal one," the young and beautiful heroine of *Look at the Harlequins!* whose only name is "Reality." Yeats's poem anticipates the movement away from sordid reality that imaginative art makes possible; Nabokov's novel celebrates the real world that saves the artist from the madness of his dreams.[2]

Such a celebration might seem at first glance to be an about-face for a writer whose work has so consistently focused on the dream—the spectacular visions of art that grow, as Yeats says, "in pure mind." But the theme of art in Nabokov's books has always had its own countertheme: the dream of art is rooted and grounded in a reality that is as complex and dazzling as the dream itself, and that finally must command the artist's most profound allegiance.[3] John Shade, Nabokov's sanest artist, knew that even the most visionary and enchanting of imagined worlds could allure only by offering a replica of ordinary, sublunary life:

And I'll turn down eternity unless
The melancholy and the tenderness
Of mortal life; the passion and the pain;
The claret taillight of that dwindling plane
Off Hesperus; your gesture of dismay
On running out of cigarettes; the way
You smile at dogs; the trail of silver slime
Snails leave on flagstones; this good ink, this rhyme,
This index card, this slender rubber band
Which always forms, when dropped, an ampersand,
Are found in Heaven by the newlydead
Stored in its strongholds through the years. [*Pale Fire*, p. 37]

The artist must be able to live in one world while he creates another, and to recognize the treacherousness of the created world of words. This necessary two-sidedness in the artist is reflected in Nabokov's explanation (complete with the parodic self-aggrandizement characteristic of his published remarks about himself) of the pseudonym under which his own work first appeared: "In modern times *sirin* is one of the popular Russian names of the Snowy Owl, the terror of tundra rodents, and is also applied to the handsome Hawk Owl, but in old Russian mythology it is a multicolored bird, with a woman's face and bust, no doubt identical with the 'siren,' a Greek deity, transporter of souls and teaser of sailors" (*Strong Opinions*, p. 161). Nabokov's madmen—Kinbote, Humbert (for part of his book), and the narrator of *Look at the Harlequins!* (for part of his book)—are mad precisely because the siren song they hear in the dream of art has lured them away from the world of "blessed matter," as

Humbert puts it, and of mortal, vulnerable, human beings. There are things in that world that the madmen miss, things as fine as anything art has to offer: the metamorphosis of a butterfly, the pattern of a bird's tracks in the snow, the sound of children at play.

Look at the Harlequins! is the fictitious autobiography of Vadim Vadimovich N., a pompous, fastidious, intermittently lecherous and usually obtuse novelist whose curriculum vitae looks enough like that of another V.V.N. to tempt the unwary to suspect that the novel may be an oblique, satiric self-portrait. Vadim Vadimovich, like Vladimir Vladimirovich, is a Russian aristocrat who was born in 1899, fled Russia at the beginning of the Bolshevist revolution, went to Cambridge, lived among other émigrés in Paris, taught literature at an American university and then left America for Switzerland, and whose novels (in Russian and English) are recognizable as muddled versions of Nabokov's. On the other hand, there are important differences: Vadim cannot remember his parents, he never lived in Berlin, he is twice widowed, once divorced, and on the verge of marrying a fourth time at the end of the book, and (N.B.) he loathes butterflies.[4] This V.V.N. is the other's look-alike, not his self-portrait; Nabokov himself remains as elusive in *Look at the Harlequins!* as he has been in all the previous novels, hovering in the background as a shadowy presence whose existence and authority—in every sense of the word—Vadim is aware of in moments when he considers the seemingly aimless meanderings of his life: "I now confess that I was bothered that night, and the next and some time before, by a dream feeling that my life was the non-identical twin, a parody, an inferior variant of another man's life, somewhere on this or another earth. A demon, I felt, was forcing me to impersonate that other man, that other writer who was and would always be incomparably greater, healthier, and crueler than your obedient servant" (p. 89). Nabokov's casting of his narrator in the role of unwilling impersonator of his incomparably greater creator is, from one point of view, a smugly arrogant move. It effectively closes off the book to readers who aren't thoroughly familiar with the life and works of Vladimir Nabokov—and to those uninterested in a character who is little more than an actor, free to improvise his lines but not to change his fixed role. *Look at the Harlequins!* is clearly a coterie book, most accessible and interesting to those already accustomed to slipping in to join "the children among you and all my old selves" (p. 123) for whom both Vadim and Nabokov stage their word shows.

The trouble that readers have had in fixing this novel is indicated by the remarks of two of its reviewers, both experienced readers of Nabokov: the first concluded that it is "undoubtedly fired by something blacker and more troubled than one is used to in Nabokov's novels," while the second found that "Nabokov's long joust and love-feast with reality seems notably good-humored in this novel."[5] Like the second reviewer, I find the book much more good-humored than troubled, but the very fact that it has produced such divergent reactions is one indication of its hermetic quality. The novel's general direction and its larger themes are clear enough, but many incidents and details remain opaque and, perhaps for that reason, seem gratuitous.

One of the central scenes in the book, which describes the death of Vadim's first wife, provides a good illustration of the problem. The scene is set in Paris, where Vadim and Iris (whose name becomes an anagram of "Sirin" when her married initial is added) are living. She has been having an affair, which Vadim suspects but does not want to acknowledge, with a Russian named Lieutenant Starov, whose name is also suggestive. Nabokov's favorite, Pushkin, fought an inconclusive duel with a Colonel Starov in 1822, and there is an incidental character named Dr. Starov in *Sebastian Knight* and one named Starover Blue in *Pale Fire*. On April 23—the birthday of Shakespeare and Nabokov—Vadim and Iris get a telephone call from her brother, Ivor Black (ivory black?) who is visiting Paris and invites them to dinner. On the way out Iris pauses before the mirror to check the "silky black bob" (p. 65) of her hair, although a few pages earlier Vadim had described the fall of her "brown curls" as she bent over "sheets of foolscap almost perforated by the violence of the violet characters that covered it" (p. 56). Much later, Vadim will mention the "chestnut-brown, violet-brown curls" of his third wife, Louise (p. 160). Ivor, Iris, and Vadim have dinner at a restaurant called the Paon d'Or, which Vadim says American tourists persist in calling the "Pander" or "Pandora." This mention of

"pander" carries over to the dinner-table conversation when
Ivor recalls his appearance ten years earlier as Cressida in a performance of Shakespeare's *Troilus and Cressida*. Iris mentions to
Ivor that she and Vadim are planning to leave Paris the next day
for Cannice. Vadim, to whom this planned removal comes as a
surprise, begins to worry that the transplantation will disrupt
his writing: "I saw my pages and notes flash past like the bright
windows of an express train that did not stop at my station"
(p. 69).

After dinner the three return home for brandy; as they walk
from the taxi to the front door Iris is suddenly approached by
Starov, who pulls out a pistol and shoots her and then himself.
Iris dies immediately, but Starov does not. He is taken to a special hospital run by a Dr. Lazareff (later in the book Vadim will
mention a young émigré poet named Lazarev). The hospital is a
"very round, mercilessly round, building on the top of a hill,
thickly covered with horse chestnut, wild rose, and other poignant plants" (p. 70). Starov lingers for weeks, and Vadim hears
from a male nurse at the hospital that in his dying delirium
Starov talked of a childhood experience that introduces another
disturbing train image. The experience Starov recalls is that of
riding on an amusement-park train which "pursued a circular
course through a brambly picturesque nightmare grove whose
dizzy flowers nodded continuous assent to all the horrors of
childhood and hell" (p. 70).

The proliferation of puzzling, seemingly unconnected details
that make up the texture of this episode is indicative of the quality of *Look at the Harlequins!* that most distinguishes it from Nabokov's other novels. *Ada* is also a very dense and allusive book,
but its referents belong to the public domain and its accumulated details coalesce around the thematic centers of the novel,
so that pursuing the allusions and figuring out the puzzles usually reward whatever effort is required. The intensely private nature of *Look at the Harlequins!* is much more problematical for the
reader; the problems, however, do not put the novel out of reach
or even keep it from being an impressively good book. (The two
reviewers I mentioned earlier were also impressed; one called it
"a magnificent novel" and the other considered it the best of Nabokov's last three books, including *Ada*.) What saves *Look at the*

Harlequins! from its potentially self-defeating obscurity is the very fact that so many of its details *are* gratuitous, or at least peripheral. The novel's story moves along at what the blurb-writer in *Ada* calls a spanking good pace, and while we must regret, and might resent, missing out on the private fun Nabokov seems to be having in the background, the front-and-center action makes for an engrossing show.

In this carnival book (the opening scenes are set in Carnavaux, France) Vadim calls all the characters from his other books back onto the stage and cavorts at the head of this "procession of my Russian and English harlequins, followed by a tiger or two, scarlet-tongued, and a libellula girl on an elephant" (p. 228). Vadim is the zany who clumsily imitates Nabokov, and his harlequins in turn mimic the people of Nabokov's books. Sebastian Knight and Mr. Goodman, Pnin, Krug, Humbert and Lolita, Van and Ada, and the major characters from the Russian novels all turn up in Vadim's novels, although they are wearing disguises and in most cases have changed their names. The one major Nabokov work that Vadim does not produce a mangled version of is the edition of *Eugene Onegin*; instead, he makes in actuality the return visit to Russia that Nabokov had to make intellectually to produce his edition. Vadim goes to Saint Petersburg in search of his runaway daughter, Bel. The details of his meeting there with Bel's Russian roommate, Dora, make sense only if one is familiar with the Nabokov commentary to *Onegin*, especially the frequent references to Byron's influence on Pushkin and the sarcastic retort to critics who find political significance everywhere in Pushkin, even in his descriptions of the weather: "One cannot afford to overlook the well-known fact that here, as in other poems, Pushkin makes an allusion to his political plight in meteorological terms" (2:188). Vadim meets Dora near the statue of Pushkin "erected some ten years before by a committee of weathermen. . . . The meteorological associations of the monument predominated over its cultural ones" (p. 211). Dora turns out to have a club foot, and for those who might miss that clue, she mentions in the course of conversation that "as a girl I dreamt of becoming a female clown, 'Madam Byron' or 'Trek Trek'" (p. 213). Incidentally, the strong ghost of Pushkin makes a number of other appearances in this novel. For instance, Vadim's second wife, Annette, was persuaded to leave him by her Sovieto-phile and puritanical friend Ninel, who considered Vadim's books decadent. The combined names of these two women point directly to Annette Olenin, a woman Pushkin was once very much in love with but who refused his proposal of marriage partly, Nabokov says in the *Onegin* commentary, because she and her family "did not relish his immoral verses" (3:206).

Dora's dream has come true, in a sense. The harlequins of Nabokov's novel—including Dora, Vadim, and his books—put on a classical pantomime show, miming with broadly comic gestures the actions of the performers in another drama taking place simultaneously.[6] In this case, however, the other show is being performed offstage; the harlequinade is a buffo commentary on a more sober performance that neither the audience nor the clowns can see. Vadim is at least vaguely aware of that other performance. He has had, since childhood, the sense of "a certain insidious and relentless connection with other states of being which were not exactly 'previous' or 'future,' but definitely out of bounds, mortally speaking" (p. 7). Vadim's life and art are burlesque versions of these other states of being—Nabokov's life and art. That is the main plot of this pantomime, but there are complicated subplots, and what emerges from the whole is a vindication of Vadim's observation that "most of life is mimodrama" (p. 123). Love and art, the two foci of Vadim's autobiography, are the two spheres of human activity that one thinks of as demanding the purest ardor, the most complete and artless surrender of the self. Yet, as Vadim suggests in referring to his subjects as "the mirages of romantic and literary matters" (p. 85), even love and art, in the public, visible forms they take the moment they are given expression, are deceptive, fatamorganic imitations of something existing out of bounds, beyond the range of logic and language.

Vadim is driven to both love and art by the need to find an objective embodiment of his desires, a perfect complement to the formless images of his imagination. The women he chooses to love, and sometimes marry, are approximations of a prototypical "latent inamorata" (p. 102) who appears periodically in his dreams as a lovely, laughing child enticing him, also a child in these dreams, to her bed, located in an unplaceable room in one of the houses of Vadim's Russian childhood. The dream is an evocation of the past and the future, of what is lost and what is only latent. Vadim, refusing to recognize the impossible remoteness of the dream image, attempts to incarnate his inamorata, and thus to bring both past and future to life in the present, by making love to the women whose images he can mentally reshape to resemble his dream-child. The ploy, of course, does not work. Vadim's three marriages and his one serious affair all begin in tedium and end in disaster. His comment on the first marriage is equally applicable to all three: "I should have been happier. I had *planned* to be happier" (p. 52). Life in the present, Vadim finds, is mocked by memory and desire, and its pleasures are only teasing approximations of remembered and anticipated joys.

The course of Vadim's love life is exactly paralleled by the course of his career in art. As a young man, a Russian writer in the first years of exile, he had a waking dream that is the professional equivalent of his erotic vision of the inamorata:

I actually believed even then, in my early twenties, that by mid-century I would be a famous and free author, living in a free, universally respected Russia, on the English quay of the Neva or on one of my splendid estates in the country, and writing there prose and poetry in the infinitely plastic tongue of my ancestors. . . . The forefeel of fame was as heady as the old wines of nostalgia. It was remembrance in reverse. . . . Why do tears blur my glasses when I invoke that phantasm of fame as it tempted and tortured me then, five decades ago? Its image was innocent, its image was genuine, its difference from what actually was to be breaks my heart like the pangs of separation. [P. 23]

This dream, like the erotic one, is an amalgam of irretrievable past and impossible future, and the love and labor that Vadim gives to the realization of the dream in the present add up to nothing more than a sorry substitute for the original, torturing image.

The pattern established in Vadim's descriptions of these mocking phantasms of love and fame is repeated in his accounts of the actual process of writing—first poems, then novels in Russian, and finally novels in English. In his early days as a poet, Vadim attempts to reproduce raw experience and raw emotion, usually love, without the buffer of a calculated style or a fictional framework.[7] He eventually abandons love poetry in favor of novels, but even these inventions are still recognizable as transfigured versions of his own experience. Vadim's art is so much a reflection of his life that he can declare in the opening pages of his autobiography that "the present memoir derives much of its value from being a *catalogue raisonné* of the roots and origins and amusing birth canals of many images in my Russian and especially English fiction" (p. 5). If the autobiography provides an entry into the art, then, by the same token, the art should help to define the man who produced it. But the pattern of the imitative harlequinade holds true once again: the art at its best is only a pantomime commentary on its unseen and ultimately unnameable source. Vadim acknowledges this truth in discussing his early struggles with poetry:

In those days I seemed to have had two muses: the essential, hysterical, genuine one, who tortured me with elusive snatches of imagery and wrung her hands over my inability to appropriate the magic and madness offered me; and her apprentice, her palette girl and stand-in, a little logician, who stuffed the torn gaps left by her mistress with explanatory or meter-mending fillers which became more and more numerous the further I moved away from the initial, evanescent, savage perfection. The treacherous music of Russian rhythms came to my specious rescue like those demons who break the black silence of an artist's hell with imitations of Greek poets and prehistorical birds. Another and final deception would come with the Fair Copy in which, for a short while, calligraphy, vellum paper, and India ink beautified a dead doggerel. [P. 44]

This description of the two muses is again evocative of the frustrating dream of the inamorata. In that dream the child across the room lures Vadim by playfully mumbling words that he cannot understand, and that he only gradually recognizes are being spoken for his benefit. The inamorata and the "essential" muse are variations of the same siren of the imagination: a temptress who has Vadim in thrall, whose erotic enchantments are inextricably bound up with her maddening offer of words he cannot quite hear, and who provides her own demotic replacements in the apprentice muse and the real women of Vadim's waking life.

The language and imagery of the description of the two muses ("savage," "stuffed," "rescue," "black silence," "deception," "dead doggerel") have a source which Vadim himself may not recognize as such, since he mentions it only much later in the book and then without relating it to the earlier passage. His estranged second wife, Annette, was killed when a tornado destroyed the house in which she and their daughter, Bel, were living. Bel survived the storm by sheltering in the basement of a museum, where her school class had been taken to see a collection of stuffed animals. Years later, Vadim discovers a poem that Bel wrote, apparently in response to that experience:

> In the dark basement, I stroked
> the silky head of a wolf.
> When the light returned
> and all cried: "Ah!,"
> it turned out to be only
> Médor, a dead dog. [P. 172]

Vadim quotes the poem without explication, but the intensity of his reaction to it is telling: "On rereading those strange lines, I see through their starry crystal the tremendous commentary I could write about them with galaxies of reference marks and footnotes like the reflections of brightly lit bridges spanning black water" (p. 172). *Look at the Harlequins!* is Vadim's commentary, in the form of an autobiographical memoir, on the savage, silent, invisible wolf at the dark center of love and art, and its daylight counterpart, a dead family pet.

In the introduction to the translation of his Russian novel *Glory*, Nabokov observed that by not making the protagonist of that novel an artist he cruelly prevented him "from finding in art—not an 'escape' (which is only a cleaner cell on a quieter floor), but relief from the itch of being!"[8] Art provides for Vadim the relief—not escape, and not cure either—that Martin Edelweiss of *Glory* is denied. Vadim, who once refers to his favorite poets and their collected works as "my dear bespangled mimes and their wands of painted lath" (p. 163), uses his art, like the traditional lath of the harlequin (*Look at the Harlequins!*) as both a magic wand and a counterfeit weapon. He needs the magic wand to transform the pure, tormenting images of the imagination into the patchwork mummers of his books, and the weapon to hold at bay the terrors of too much reality. The lath is, however, in both cases only a temporary expedient. In the first place, the language of his art, no matter which language he uses, is frustratingly limited; his words can never quite catch up with the most shadowy and disturbing of the lurking figures of the imagination. Near the end of his memoir Vadim recounts pausing, shortly before his seventy-first birthday, to take stock of all that he has written so far. He is satisfied with his Russian output, because by switching to English he arbitrarily put an end to his career as a Russian writer. "That Russian batch of my books was finished and signed and thrust back into the mind that had produced them. . . . That was settled." All's well that ends, apparently. The novels in English, on the other hand, are not finished, and Vadim is troubled by what is missing from them: "I knew I would always keep hoping that my *next* book—not simply the one in progress, like *Ardis*—but something I had never attempted yet, something miraculous and unique, would at last answer fully the craving, the aching thirst that a few disjunct paragraphs in *Esmeralda* and *The Kingdom* were insufficient to quench" (p. 229). The itch, to shift the metaphor just a bit, is clearly still there.

Vadim also uses his art to defend himself against truths he does not want to recognize and emotions he is afraid of succumbing to. For instance, "the monastic rules of work on my novella" (p. 61) divert his attention from the growing suspicion—a correct one, as it turns out—that his first wife has a lover, and when that lover murders her the distraught Vadim finds his only consolation in "the colored phrase in my mind under the drizzle, the white page under the desk lamp" (p. 79). Similarly, when he begins to realize that his adored Bel is slipping away from him forever, he assuages the pain of those "dark years of my heart" by beginning a new novel—an oblique account of his love for Bel (recognizable to the reader as a clumsy imitation of *Lolita*). "Its demands, the fun and fancy of it, its intricate imagery, made up in a way for the absence of my beloved Bel" (p. 193). Vadim holds off his grief for a while by translating it into the stuff of a fanciful novel. The fact of Bel's departure from his life, however, cannot be changed, and he must eventually confront the agony of a final farewell, even though he is "dying, trying to turn everything into a dream, a dream about that last hideous moment" (p. 196). The artist's weapon fails him when he needs it most, to save him from the very real pain of loss and remorse.

Vadim's autobiography, his story of love and art, is the record of a pattern of failures, fresh starts, and more failures: the outer reality consistently turns out to be a clumsy imitation of the inner, imagined reality, and yet the vague images of the imagination keep driving Vadim to seek their embodiment in the perfect woman and the perfectly articulated work of art. That pattern changes, however, in the final pages of the book, and the pantomime show of *Look at the Harlequins!* concludes with the obligatory transformation scene and happy ending. The agent of change is another woman, different from the others because she stumbles into Vadim's life unexpectedly, before the vision of the latent inamorata has a chance to presage her arrival, and because she has the solution to a problem that has threatened him with insanity all his life. The problem, as he explains it to each of his wives and finally to his new, last love, seems quite simple: he cannot imagine the physical process of turning his body around to change directions.

In actual, physical life I can turn as simply and swiftly as anyone. But mentally, with my eyes closed and my body immobile, I am unable to switch from one direction to the other. Some swivel cell in my brain does not work. I can cheat, of course, by setting aside the mental snapshot of one vista and leisurely selecting the opposite view for my walk back to my starting point. But if I do not cheat, some kind of atrocious obstacle, which would drive me mad if I persevered, prevents me from imagining the twist which transforms one direction into another, directly opposite. I am crushed, I am carrying the whole world on my back in the process of trying to visualize my turning around and making myself see in terms of "right" what I saw in terms of "left" and vice versa. [Pp. 41–42]

The problem becomes more than hypothetical when Vadim, in the course of an evening stroll, suddenly finds that his body will not make the pivot that his imagination had refused to make so many times before; he cannot turn around. Vadim collapses, remains in a coma for three weeks, then gradually regains his senses and his awareness of who and where he is. His full recovery, which amounts almost to a resurrection, is signaled by his joyous recognition of the woman he loves, whose only name in this memoir is the emblematic one Vadim gives her: "I emitted a bellow of joy, and Reality entered" (p. 250).

This woman, this "Reality," knows the answer to the puzzle that Vadim has explained to three other women, his wives, and that has made him feel that he might lose his reason at any moment. His mistake, she tells him, is that he has confused space and time, direction and duration. To imagine taking a walk is to collect impressions that "refer to a series of time events, and not to blocks of painted space that a child can rearrange in any old way." She does not find it surprising, then, that he cannot make that mental pivot: "Nobody can imagine in physical terms the act of reversing the order of time. Time is not reversible. Reverse motion is used in films only for comic effects" (pp. 252–53). Such a simple explanation is, as Vadim protests, "merely an exquisite quibble" (p. 253), but it is enough: he is cured.

Vadim's recovery from his "dementia paralytica" marks an equally healthy and auspicious recovery from the emotional paralysis that has characterized his life. By awakening to greet "Reality" with a shout of joy and by recognizing the logical impossibility of trying to reverse time mentally, Vadim has in effect banished the latent inamorata who taunted him with images from a dead past and an impossible future, and who by her very presence made the real women in his life appear to him as poor imitations of her innocence, purity, and perfection. Vadim learns, in time to assure a happy ending to his book, what Humbert Humbert learns too late—that only art is free to reshuffle time and space, that the innocent nymphets of memory and imagination sometimes breed live monsters, and that the dream visions of art can lure the dreamer away from the profound, enduring, and literally unspeakable joys of the here and now.

Among the many dates that pedantic Vadim carefully notes in his text, there are two that are particularly relevant to the happy but abrupt ending he has given to this otherwise melancholy account of his life. Early in the book he identifies "nowadays" as 1970 (p. 52), but a hundred pages later "the moment of writing" has become February 15, 1974 (p. 168). The events occurring in that four-year interval—which include Vadim's attack, his recovery, and the solving of the time-space puzzle—have so changed the direction and tenor of his life that the design of the autobiography is no longer workable. In one of his early chapters Vadim pauses for a parenthetical observation about the structure of his book:

In this memoir my wives and my books are interlaced monogrammatically like some sort of watermark or *ex libris* design; and in writing this oblique autobiography—oblique, because dealing mainly not with pedestrian history but with the mirages of romantic and literary matters—I consistently try to dwell as lightly as inhumanly possible on the evolution of my mental illness. Yet Dementia is one of the characters in my story. [P. 85]

In the early portions of the book the interlacing of love and art has become so much a habit of mind for Vadim that he frequently describes lovemaking in stylistic terms and writing in sexual terms. In recalling his life with Iris, for example, he mentions "inflections of lovemaking, felicities of fondling, the easy accuracy with which she adapted her flexible frame to every pattern of passion" (p. 53). His description of dictating sessions with his first typist, the beautiful and adoring Lyubov Serafimovna Savich, is especially revealing:

As a typist L. S. was magnificent. Hardly had I finished dictating one sentence, as I paced back and forth, than it had reached her furrow like a handful of grain, and with one eyebrow raised she was already looking at me, waiting for the next strewing. If a sudden alteration for the better occurred to me in mid-session, I preferred not to spoil the wonderful give-and-take rhythm of our joint work by introducing painful pauses of word weighing—especially enervating and sterile when a self-conscious author is aware that the bright lady at the waiting typewriter is longing to come up with a helpful suggestion. [P. 82]

By the end of the book all that has changed. Love and art have become disentangled in Vadim's mind, Dementia has consequently been removed from the cast, and the pedestrian history that Vadim skipped over so lightly has become the "Reality" that he welcomes with a bellow of joy. Once Vadim has accounted for these dramatic reversals, there is nothing more for the auto-biography to do except to stop, as it does, in mid-sentence.

The autobiography ends, ironically, just where Vadim's "real life" begins, but in the failure of the design of the memoir the intricate design of Nabokov's novel becomes apparent. Vadim cannot describe his new life, cannot give the source of his joy any name other than Reality, because to speak of it would be to change it: "Reality would only be adulterated if I now started to narrate what you know, what I know, what nobody else knows, what shall never, never be ferreted out by a matter-of-fact, father-of-muck, mucking biograffitist" (p. 226). Vadim Vadimovich N., like Sebastian Knight and, more important, like the other V.V.N. he resembles, escapes through the back door of his art. The real life of the artist will not be found in his books, not even in his autobiography; the deceptive figures of those books perform a metaphoric harlequinade that is finally no more than commentary on something that—although it claims his profoundest love—remains inaccessible to his art, and thus beyond the reach of writer and reader.

"We free ourselves from obsession that we may be nothing," Yeats wrote in a letter. "The last kiss is given to the void."[9] Nabokov's Vadim frees himself from obsession to become what is in the world of Nabokov's fiction the most enviable of all things—a sane, healthy, loved and loving mortal—and his last kiss is given to the woman who saves him from the void, the woman who goes by the name of "Reality."

It is appropriate in several ways that this novel, the most affirmative of any that Nabokov wrote, should be the last one that he published during his lifetime. Whether he intended to or not, and I suspect that he did, Nabokov provided in *Look at the Harlequins!* a final, authoritative retrospective on both his professional career and his private life. This last novel is clearly a summing up, a reiteration of old themes, a reaffirmation of old beliefs, and a celebration of old loves. It is also the most personal of the novels, first because it is the most eccentric and esoteric, and second because it contains the most recognizable fragments of Nabokov's private and professional lives. At the same time, this is the book in which he most emphatically insists that the man and the picture of the man that emerges from the books are not the same. There is also the matter of the ending—the most unambiguously happy one in the English novels. It is as if Nabokov were preempting that perceptive "reappraiser" he once predicted might come along some day and set the record straight by declaring that Nabokov was in fact an optimist and moralist all along (*Strong Opinions*, p. 193).

Finally, the fact that the final scene of this novel is set in California, in the late afternoon of a June day, seems telling in the light of Nabokov's remark that "frequently, especially in the spring, I dream of going to spend my purple-plumed sunset in California" (*Strong Opinions*, p. 124).

There is other evidence, outside of *Look at the Harlequins!*, that Nabokov may have intended this book to be a clearing up of promises made to himself and a public valediction to the practice of his art. At the end of his last Russian novel, *The Gift*, the protagonist Fyodor and his fiancée Zina have a discussion in which Fyodor speaks of the things he would like to accomplish as a writer and the sort of finish he envisions for his life. He has been reminiscing with Zina about the deceptiveness of fate in finally bringing them together by "a last desperate maneuver" after three abortive attempts to make their paths cross (like Vadim's three abortive marriages):

"Now isn't that the plot for a remarkable novel? What a theme! But it must be built up, curtained, surrounded by dense life— my life, my professional passions and cares."

"Yes, but that will result in an autobiography with mass ex-
ecutions of good acquaintances."

"Well, let's suppose that I so shuffle, twist, mix, rechew and
rebelch everything, add such spices of my own and impregnate
things so much with myself that nothing remains of the autobiography but dust—the kind of dust, of course, which makes
the most orange of skies. And I shan't write it now, I'll be a
long time preparing it, years perhaps . . . In any case I'll do
something else first—I want to translate something in my own
manner from an old French sage—in order to reach a final dictatorship over words." [P. 376]

Fyodor then abruptly switches the subject and begins to recite
for Zina a story from the work of the sage he wants to translate:

"There was once a man . . . ; he lived a pure, difficult, wise life;
but when he sensed the approach of death, instead of thinking
about it, instead of tears of repentance and sorrowful partings,
instead of monks and a notary in black, he invited guests to a
feast, acrobats, actors, poets, a crowd of dancing girls, three
magicians, jolly Tollenburg students, a traveler from Tap-
robana, and in the midst of melodious verses, masks and
music he drained a goblet of wine and died, with a carefree
smile on his face. . . . Magnificent, isn't it? If I have to die one
day that's exactly how I'd like it to be." [P. 377]

Look at the Harlequins! fulfills both of Fyodor's wishes at once. It is
an autobiography rechewed, rebelched, and reduced to dust,
and it is the gayest and most celebratory of Nabokov's books, in
which acrobats and actors have been invited to share a lively
parting feast.

There is one other important way in which this last book
seems both a fitting departure from the other novels and a fitting final comment on all of them. Like the rest of Nabokov's
protagonists, Vadim Vadimovich N. clings tenaciously to the
notion that his life is authored by someone smarter and more
farseeing than he is, because, like the others, he sees in the pur-
posiveness and completeness of fictional lives an inviting alternative to the apparent shapelessness of his own. Convinced of

the supremacy of the text, he is therefore as passionate about his annotations and as obsessive about his allusions as any of the others, and his book suggests that he is just as convinced as they are that "the alchemy of a scholium" *can* unlock the secrets of a universe. The important difference between Vadim and the others is that he is the only one who comes to understand fully (and gratefully) that the universe of the texts he reads or writes or annotates is not the one in which he lives. He overcomes, at last, the lust to footnote his own life.

Like most novels, Nabokov's end just at the point at which the major character has exhausted his ability to interest us further without a massive restructuring of his situation. This final novel ends with the character's exhilarating and liberating recognition that he is not defined by a text—his or anyone else's. Vadim in effect exchanges his status as character for that of reader and writer. If that means for us that he becomes less interesting, it means for him that he can exult in his ordinariness, his limitations, his freedom to be human. For these reasons, it is appropriate that Vadim should end his book mumbling drowsily and incoherently about tea laced with rum, since in the world to which he has awakened from the nightmare of near-death and near-madness, a world dominated by "Reality" and not by the aesthetic and formal demands of a text, rum and dreamless sleep are among the choicest pleasures, and incoherence is no crime.

Notes

Introduction

1. Two other readers of Nabokov have offered similar observations. John O. Lyons (*"Pale Fire* and the Fine Art of Annotation," in *Nabokov: The Man and His Work*, ed. L. S. Dembo [Madison: University of Wisconsin Press, 1967], pp. 157–64) describes Nabokov's "favorite narrative method, which is the examination of a text (or vision of aesthetic order) by some real or imagined artist who vies with God in disordering a universe" (p. 157). Lyons finds the method working in only three novels, *The Real Life of Sebastian Knight*, *Lolita*, and *Pale Fire*, and concentrates on the structural similarities between these novels and two actual commentaries, Nabokov's notes to *Eugene Onegin* and Pope's notes on *The Dunciad*. Clarence Brown, in his excellent "Nabokov's Pushkin and Nabokov's Nabokov," also in the Dembo volume (pp. 195–208), observes that "the poem-and-commentary form is the essential structure of the novels *The Real Life of Sebastian Knight*, *The Gift*, and even *The Defense*" (p. 205). Since Brown's real subject is the *Onegin* commentary, however, his remarks about the novels are summary and brief.
2. The extent to which the moral sense of Nabokov's characters con-

tributes to their motivation, and to the thematic configurations of the novels, has been the subject of much critical debate since the publication of Lionel Trilling's now-famous essay on *Lolita*, "The Last Lover," *Encounter* 11 (October 1958): 9–19. The range of positions taken by those who have continued the debate is suggested by comparing Robert M. Adams's assertion that "Nabokov's world consists of flats, facades, transparencies; as for the moral and humane dimensions—'profundities', compassions, inner developments—it simply does not have them" with Douglas Fowler's equally unequivocal conclusion that "in Nabokov's worlds, to have consciousness is to be *morally* conscious." See Adams, "Fiction Chronicle," *Hudson Review* 15 (Autumn 1962): 423; Fowler, *Reading Nabokov* (Ithaca, N.Y.: Cornell University Press, 1974), p. 95. Others who have contributed to the debate include Martin Green, "The Morality of *Lolita*," *Kenyon Review* 28 (June 1966): 352–77; Alfred Appel, Jr., "*Lolita*: The Springboard of Parody," in *Nabokov*, ed. Dembo; Bobbie Ann Mason, *Nabokov's Garden: A Guide to Ada* (Ann Arbor, Mich.: Ardis, 1974); Mark Lilly, "Nabokov: Homo Ludens," in *Vladimir Nabokov: A Tribute*, ed. Peter Quennell (New York: Morrow, 1980); Ellen Pifer, *Nabokov and the Novel* (Cambridge: Harvard University Press, 1980).

Chapter I

1. One indication of how alien the American landscape is to Kinbote appears in his description of an evening stroll with Shade—a man who, Kinbote knows, likes and respects those people who know "the names of things" in the natural environment. The walk, as Kinbote describes it, takes them past "flowering dogwoods" and then to "the top of the hill, where a square plot invaded with willow herb, milkweed and ironweed, and teeming with butterflies, contrasted sharply with the goldenrod all around it" (pp. 185, 186). Of the plants Kinbote names, some bloom in the spring, some in midsummer, and some in the late summer; since Kinbote has them all conveniently flowering simultaneously, and since their names are all indicative of the kind of nomenclatorial plainness, the lack of associative magic, that Kinbote finds so puzzling about the American language, his description seems a bold and blundering attempt to sound not only like an American, but like one who is comfortable in his knowledge of "the names of things."
2. William Butler Yeats, "William Blake and the Imagination," in *Essays and Introductions* (New York: Collier, 1961), p. 114.

3. Nikolai Gogol, *The Diary of a Madman and Other Stories*, trans. Andrew R. MacAndrew (New York: Signet, 1960), pp. 20–21.
4. Andrew Field was, I believe, the first to point out that "*izumrud* means 'emerald' in Russian" (*Nabokov: His Life in Art* [Boston: Little, Brown, 1967], p. 312).
5. See, for example, Field, *Nabokov: His Life in Art*; Julia Bader, *Crystal Land: Artifice in Nabokov's English Novels* (Berkeley and Los Angeles: University of California Press, 1972); Green, "Morality of *Lolita*." Both Field and Bader argue that Kinbote and Shade are extensions of two aspects of a single self. Bader also concludes that the ending of *The Real Life of Sebastian Knight* demonstrates "the inescapable oneness of Sebastian and V" (p. 14), and Field argues that in *Lolita* Clare Quilty "has no life apart from Humbert's will" (p. 348). Green contends that two of the secondary characters in *Lolita*, Quilty and John Ray, Jr., are the inventions of Humbert Humbert. One problem with this kind of reading of the novels is suggested by Bader's repeated insistence that the "inexpert" reader will misinterpret the books by failing to recognize the multiple levels of their duplicity. Bader's book, on the other hand, seems to me an instance of the tendency of the "expert" reader to overinterpret by assuming that every premise in the novels is ironic and every situation a potential trap for the naive, so that the critic must demonstrate his own inventiveness and sly ingenuity before he can be considered a reliable guide to the novels.
6. James Boswell, *Boswell's Life of Johnson* (New York: Oxford University Press, 1960), pp. 343, 107.
7. Ibid., p. 22.
8. Ibid., p. 979.

Chapter II

1. The "white widowed male," as the fictitious editor John Ray, Jr., tags Humbert Humbert, appears frequently among Nabokov's major characters. In addition to K and Humbert, Adam Krug of *Bend Sinister*, Hugh Person of *Transparent Things*, and Vadim Vadimovich N. of *Look at the Harlequins!* are all widowers, as are a number of characters in the short stories. There are hints in *Pale Fire* that Charles Kinbote may also be among this group.
2. Apparently Kinbote's disorientation was literally fatal, according to a remark Nabokov made in 1966: "I think it is so nice that the day on which Kinbote committed suicide (and he certainly did after putting the last touches to his edition of the poem) happens to be both

the anniversary of Pushkin's *Lyceum* and that of 'poor old man Swift''s death" (*Strong Opinions*, p. 74).

3. There is a passing reference to *The Real Life of Sebastian Knight* in *Speak, Memory* which suggests that one source of the novel might be traced to Nabokov's feelings about his homosexual younger brother, Sergey, who died in a German concentration camp in 1945: "For various reasons I find it inordinately hard to speak about my other brother. That twisted quest for Sebastian Knight (1940) with its gloriettes and self-mate combinations, is really nothing in comparison with the task I balked in the first version of this memoir and am faced with now. . . . He is a mere shadow in the background of my richest and most detailed recollections" (p. 190).

   Nabokov (wiser, less obsessed, and more discreet than his character V) in effect balks the task again. He devotes four brief paragraphs to noting the few points at which his life and Sergey's crossed paths, and then concludes that Sergey's is "one of those lives that hopelessly claim a belated something—compassion, understanding, no matter what—which the mere recognition of such a want can neither replace nor redeem" (p. 191). If Nabokov was thinking of himself and Sergey when he wrote the novel, he may have attempted to distance himself from the subject, which he clearly felt strongly about, by reversing the roles of Vladimir and Sergey in the portrayal of V and Sebastian. In *Sebastian Knight* the shadowy brother is the novelist, and it is V, not Sebastian, whose attitude toward women raises the suspicion that he may be homosexual.

4. Nabokov, *The Waltz Invention* (New York: Phedra, 1966), p. iii.

5. Dabney Stuart identifies the "pale wretch" as V himself: "The policy of oppression has been implicitly denounced by the narrator in his account of the family's flight from revolution-torn Russia" (*Nabokov: The Dimensions of Parody* [Baton Rouge: Louisiana State University Press, 1978], p. 23).

6. My conclusion that *Sebastian Knight* fails as a novel is distinctly a minority opinion. For a selection of more admiring views, see Page Stegner, *Escape into Aesthetics: The Art of Vladimir Nabokov* (New York: Dial Press, 1966); Bader, *Crystal Land*; George M. Hyde, *Vladimir Nabokov* (London: Marion Boyars, 1977); Herbert Grabes, *Fictitious Biographies* (The Hague: Mouton, 1977); Stuart, *Nabokov*; Charles Nicol, "The Mirrors of Sebastian Knight," in *Nabokov*, ed. Dembo, pp. 85–94.

Chapter III

1. Oscar Wilde, *The Artist as Critic: Critical Writings of Oscar Wilde*, ed. Richard Ellmann (New York: Random House, 1968), p. 305.
2. *Strong Opinions*, p. 64. Nabokov expressed a stronger, less complicated opinion of James in a 1941 letter to Edmund Wilson, after Nabokov had read *The Aspern Papers* on Wilson's recommendation: "The style is artistic but it is not the style of an artist. . . . He has charm (as the weak blond prose of Turgenev has), but that's about it." See *The Nabokov-Wilson Letters, 1940–1971*, ed. Simon Karlinsky (New York: Harper and Row, n.d.), p. 53.
3. Wilde, *Artist as Critic*, p. 295.
4. Henry James, *The Art of Fiction* (New York: Oxford University Press, 1948), p. 55.
5. Wilde, *Artist as Critic*, p. 301.
6. Nabokov's initial hatred of the Soviets did not diminish over the years. These remarks were made in a 1965 interview:

   The primitive and banal mentality of enforced politics—any politics—can only produce primitive and banal art. This is especially true of the so-called "social realist" and "proletarian" literature sponsored by the Soviet police state. Its jackbooted baboons have gradually exterminated the really talented authors, the special individual, the fragile genius. . . . Tyrants and torturers will never manage to hide their comic stumbles behind their cosmic acrobatics. Contemptuous laughter is all right, but it is not enough in the way of moral relief. And when I read Mandelshtam's poems composed under the accursed rule of those beasts, I felt a kind of helpless shame, being so free to live and think and write and speak in the free part of the world.—That's the only time when liberty is bitter. [*Strong Opinions*, p. 58]

7. Edmund Wilson had similar reservations about *Bend Sinister*, which he expressed in a letter to Nabokov (January 30, 1947): "As it is, what you are left with on your hands is a satire on events so terrible that they really can't be satirized—because in order to satirize anything you have to make it worse than it is." See *Nabokov-Wilson Letters*, p. 183.
8. Howard Nemerov, *Poetry and Fiction* (New Brunswick, N.J.: Rutgers University Press, 1963), p. 265.
9. *Poems and Problems*, p. 11.

10. Frank Kermode, *Puzzles and Epiphanies* (New York: Chilmark Press, 1962), p. 232.

11. For two different interpretations of the narrator's rescue of Krug, see Pifer, *Nabokov and the Novel* and Susan Fromberg Schaeffer, "*Bend Sinister* and the Novelist as Anthropomorphic Deity," *Centennial Review* 17 (Spring 1973): 115–51. Pifer finds very positive moral and political implications in the narrator's gesture, seeing it as a sign of the individual's ability to liberate himself from tyranny by affirming "his own identity and the freedom of conscious life. . . . No matter what Paduk's regime does to torture Krug, it cannot extinguish the light of his consciousness" (p. 93). Schaeffer, on the other hand, sees the rescue as a significant structural device that is consistent with the patterns of recurrent imagery in the novel; both are, she contends, part of a Nabokovian argument from design that is unambiguous and unqualified: "In the novel, Nabokov argues that we are all characters in the vast work of an ultimate artificer whose palette is the universe and whose pigments are all things under the sun. This concept of existence underlies and explains every aspect of the novel" (p. 135). Even if we were to concede that Nabokov "argues" for anything in his novels, and that would be a very difficult concession, it is clear that most of Nabokov's protagonists, including Krug, are fully and nervously aware of the *possibility* that their world is designed, and that it is the obsession with this very possibility, which Nabokov repeatedly suggests *may be* divinest sense, that often ends in much madness. Nabokov's sanest characters are, always, those who are capable of being content with tantalizing possibilities.

12. Kermode, *Puzzles and Epiphanies*, p. 232. See also Fowler, *Reading Nabokov*, p. 56: the *Hamlet* digression is "extraneous matter created and kept for its own sake," an example of Nabokov's habit of "including sources of interest and amusement that are quasi-narrative or extranarrative"; Pifer, *Nabokov and the Novel*, p. 7: the digression is an example of Shakespeare's genius for "forging the particles of language into vital human images, metaphors embodying the distinct qualities of human life within a verbal matrix"; Strother Purdy, "Solus Rex: Nabokov and the Chess Novel," *Modern Fiction Studies* 14 (1968): 388: Krug and Emer are actually playing *Hamlet*, "with Krug as the over-thoughtful procrastinator, whose final move against the usurper Claudius-Paduk costs him his own life as well as the lives of others."

13. L. L. Lee, "*Bend Sinister*: Nabokov's Political Dream," in *Nabokov*, ed. Dembo, pp. 95–105.

14. George Steiner, "Extraterritorial," in *Nabokov: Criticism, Reminis-*

cences, Translations, and Tributes, ed. Alfred Appel, Jr., and Charles Newman (Evanston, Ill.: Northwestern University Press, 1970), pp. 123–24.

Chapter IV

1. Martha Banta, "Benjamin, Edgar, Humbert, and Jay," *Yale Review* 60 (1971): 532–49; Alfred Appel, Jr., ed., *The Annotated* Lolita (New York: McGraw-Hill, 1970), p. xxi; F. W. Dupee, "A Preface to *Lolita*," *Anchor Review* 2 (1957): 11; Leslie Fiedler, "The Profanation of the Child," *New Leader* 23 (June 1958): 26–29; Bader, *Crystal Land,* p. 64.
2. Edgar Allan Poe, *The Complete Tales and Poems of Edgar Allan Poe* (New York: Modern Library, 1938), pp. 893–94.
3. See, for example, Appel's introduction to *Annotated* Lolita, pp. 330–33; Carl R. Proffer, *Keys to* Lolita (Bloomington: Indiana University Press, 1968), pp. 34–35; Hyde, *Vladimir Nabokov,* pp. 117–18; Stegner, *Escape into Aesthetics,* pp. 105–6.
4. Poe, *Complete Tales and Poems,* pp. 656, 665.
5. John Keats, *Selected Poems and Letters,* ed. Douglas Bush (Boston: Riverside Press, 1959), p. 258.
6. Marcel Proust, *The Past Recaptured,* trans. Andreas Mayor (New York: Vintage Books, 1971), p. 138.
7. Marcel Proust, *The Captive,* trans. C. K. Scott Moncrieff (New York: Vintage Books, 1970), p. 130.
8. For other discussions of the relationship between Nabokov's fiction and Proust's, see Field, *Nabokov: His Life in Art,* pp. 343–47; Alex de Jonge, "Nabokov's Use of Pattern," in *Vladimir Nabokov,* ed. Quennell, pp. 59–72; Yvette Louria, "Nabokov and Proust: The Challenge of Time," *Books Abroad* 48 (Summer 1974): 469–76; J. E. Rivers, "Proust, Nabokov and *Ada*," *French American Review* 1 (1977): 173–97.
9. Mark Lilly ("Nabokov," in *Vladimir Nabokov,* ed. Quennell, pp. 88–102) reaches exactly the opposite conclusion. Lilly argues that the ambiguities in *Lolita* "direct us away from morality altogether, and towards the specially enchanted world where the logic and delight of games replace everyday reality" (p. 96). Given this reading, Nabokov would then seem to be encouraging the reader to adopt precisely the attitude that makes Clare Quilty so reprehensible, and the attitude that nearly destroys Humbert.
10. Henry Adams, *The Education of Henry Adams* (New York: Modern Library, n.d.), p. 268.
11. It is also possible to see the "Gerontion" allusion as two-edged; that

is, Nabokov may well have intended to suggest a comparison between Humbert and the Christ of Eliot's poem, as well as to call up
Adams's description of his reaction to the Maryland spring. Eliot's
avenger, for example, comes "swaddled in darkness"; he is "Christ
the tiger" who finally "springs," devouring the tenants of a "de-
cayed house." Humbert, in his murder of Quilty, also comes as an
avenger, dressed entirely in black. He stalks Quilty through his
"decrepit house" (p. 295), describing his step as "springy—too
springy perhaps for success. But my heart pounded with tiger joy"
(p. 297). While Humbert is clearly not a consistent Christ figure in
the novel, he does have his moment of moral housecleaning when
he kills Quilty, a moment that is necessary for his own mental and
spiritual equilibrium.

12. Nabokov's opinion of Flaubert's novel is indicated in a passage in
Speak, Memory. After his father's death, Nabokov recalls, "A fellow
student of his, with whom he had gone for a bicycle trip in the
Black Forest, sent my widowed mother the *Madame Bovary* volume
which my father had had with him at the time and on the flyleaf of
which he had written 'The unsurpassed pearl of French literature'—a judgment that still holds" (p. 129).

13. Gustave Flaubert, *Madame Bovary*, trans. Paul de Man (New York:
W. W. Norton, 1965), pp. 254–55.

14. Martin Green has suggested, appropriately, that the term *rococo realism* is a useful way of describing both the combination of ridicu-
lousness and glamor that characterizes Nabokov's vision of America in *Lolita* and the equally paradoxical combination of disgust and
celebration that characterizes Humbert Humbert's narrative style.
See "American Rococo: Nabokov and Salinger," in *Re-appraisals:
Some Commonsense Readings in American Literature* (London: Hugh
Evelyn, 1963), pp. 211–29.

Chapter V

1. *The Song of Igor's Campaign*, p. 12.
2. Douglas Fowler makes a similar observation: "This 'mad' concern
with the preposterous, 'inane' facts of time and death is perhaps
the central impulse behind Nabokov's habitual creation of the second world we find in his fiction." On the other hand, I disagree
with many of Fowler's ideas about the fate of characters in the "second world" of the novels; clearly, I do not agree with his conclusion
that "unlike Krug, Pnin has no one above him to take care of him."
See *Reading Nabokov*, pp. 15, 145.

3. "On a Book Entitled *Lolita*," appended to *Lolita*, p. 327.
4. Arthur Schnitzler, *Anatol and Other Plays*, trans. Grace Isabel Colbron (New York: Modern Library, 1925), p. 167.
5. Schnitzler, *Anatol and Other Plays*, p. 217.
6. Donald E. Morton, *Vladimir Nabokov* (New York: Frederick Unger, 1974), p. 101; Ambrose Gordon, Jr., "The Double Pnin," in *Nabokov*, ed. Dembo, p. 156; Stegner, *Escape into Aesthetics*, p. 97; Stuart, *Nabokov*, pp. 160–61.
7. Field, *Nabokov: His Life in Art*, pp. 135–36; Bader, *Crystal Land*, p. 82.
8. Even the narrator's geography is suspicious. He says, for example, that he emerges from the Cockerells' house and begins his morning walk by turning left and walking northward; before he turns, however, he notices a tall poplar tree that "rose on my right, and its long morning shadow crossing to the opposite side of the street reached there a crenulated, cream-colored house" (p. 190). The narrator's painstaking recreation of the scene thus has the early-morning sun performing a miraculous reversal and casting a long shadow from west to east.
9. In the *Eugene Onegin* commentary Nabokov refers in passing to the Russian novelist Pavel Melnikov, whose "ethnographical novel *In the Woods* . . . describes some curious blends of pagan tradition and Christian ritual existing among Russian peasants in the woodlands of the Kostroma and Nizhni-Novgorod provinces" (2:301).
10. Marcel Proust, *Swann's Way*, trans. C. K. Scott Moncrieff (New York: Vintage Books, 1970), p. 54.
11. Dabney Stuart, who takes a position that is in many ways the opposite of my own, argues that the narrator's strength is not in his attraction to Pnin, but in his ability to reject him, to exorcise the "possible alternative" he has envisioned. Stuart sees Pnin as essentially a passive victim, and finds that "the moral value of the experience of the novel lies in the narrator's choice of refusing to play that role himself." See *Nabokov*, p. 160.

Chapter VI

1. The image of the patterned carpet also appears in "The Paris Poem," which Nabokov wrote in Russian in 1943 and later translated for inclusion in *Poems and Problems* (p. 123):

> In this life, rich in patterns (a life
> unrepeatable, since with a different

cast, in a different manner,
in a new theatre it will be given),

no better joy would I choose than to fold
its magnificent carpet in such a fashion
as to make the design of today coincide
with the past, with a former pattern.

2. Bobbie Ann Mason, in her book *Nabokov's Garden*, sees Ada's various love affairs as attempts to escape the "unnaturalness" of her incestuous affair with Van and return to the "natural" world by way of a more normal sexual liaison. Mason further argues that Ada fails in this attempt because she has been victimized by Van, who "doesn't consider that he is at fault in having corrupted Ada, leaving her emotionally stunted by incest, incapable of achieving a fulfilling life, and that her loss of vitality and increased artificiality are the effects of her relationship with Van" (pp. 63–64). The argument of her book rests on the assertion that Van, as narrator, has deliberately distorted the history of his past because he is "tormented by guilt and fear that his behavior was unnatural" (p. 13), and that his entire account is a failed attempt to "justify and rationalize his incestuous life, which was responsible not only for the suffering and suicide of Lucette, but for Ada's loss of vitality, a condition to which Van is blind" (p. 23). Mason's argument seems to me overingenious and finally indefensible, although in the course of making it she provides many invaluable glosses on some of the most abstruse details in the novel.

3. Compare Robert Alter, "Nabokov's Ardor," *Commentary* 48 (August 1969): 48: "Van Veen's story represents . . . a reversal of the major thematic movement of the novel as a genre. The novel characteristically has concerned itself with lost illusions. . . . *Ada*, in direct contrast, is an attempt to return to paradise, to establish, in fact, the luminous vision of youth and love's first fulfillment as the most intensely, perdurably *real* experience we know."

4. Nathaniel Hawthorne, *The Complete Novels and Selected Tales of Nathaniel Hawthorne* (New York: Modern Library, n.d.), p. 105.

5. Proust, *Past Recaptured*, p. 133.

6. *Ada's* parodies of novelistic technique have been enumerated by others; the fullest description of them is in Alfred Appel's "*Ada* Described," in *Nabokov*, ed. Appel and Newman, pp. 160–86.

7. This reference itself might be called ambidextrous. It appears in the following sentence, which is part of Van's essay "The Texture of Time": " 'Space is a swarming in the eyes, and Time a singing in the

ears,' says John Shade, a modern poet, as quoted by an invented philosopher ('Martin Gardiner') in *The Ambidextrous Universe*, page 165" (p. 577). It is not surprising to find that there is a slight asymmetry between Van's citation and its actual, terrestrial source. The real Martin Gardner (who spells his name without the *i*) quotes the line about space and time, which is taken from the poem by Nabokov's invented poet, on page 168 of his *The Ambidextrous Universe* (New York: Basic Books, 1964). Interestingly, Gardner's identification of the source of the quoted lines is as playfully deceptive as Nabokov's: "From Canto 2 of *Pale Fire*," his footnote reads, "a poem by John Francis Shade." There is no mention of Nabokov, either in this note or in the index to the book.

8. George Steiner, "Extraterritorial," in *Nabokov*, ed. Appel and Newman, p. 124.

9. For a fairly lengthy listing of the correspondences between *Ada* and Chateaubriand's *René; ou, les effets des passions*, see Robert Alter, "*Ada*; or, The Perils of Paradise," in *Vladimir Nabokov*, ed. Quennell, pp. 103–18.

10. Nabokov's brief description of Van's difficulties is reminiscent of much that Susanne K. Langer has to say in her sustained discussion of the emotional content of art in *Feeling and Form* (New York: Scribners, 1953). The following passage seems especially relevant (particularly in its language) to Nabokov's depiction of Van Veen's problem with writing about strong personal feelings: "This brings us to the problem of 'self-expression' in a new and deepened form: not the subjective interpretation that makes art a vehicle for the performer's personal anxieties and moods, but the element of *ardor for the import conveyed*. This, of course, is actual feeling: . . . it is the contagious excitement of the artist over the vital content of the work. Where it is missing, the symbol is 'cold.' But, being an actual and not virtual phenomenon, artistic 'warmth' can never be planned and assured by any technical device. It shows itself in the final product, but always as an unconscious factor" (p. 141).

11. *The Gay Science*, sec. 381.

Chapter VII

1. *The Real Life of Sebastian Knight*, p. 204; *Pnin*, p. 135; *Lolita*, p. 311; *Pale Fire*, p. 49.

2. D. Barton Johnson, "Nabokov as Man of Letters: The Alphabetic Motif in His Work," *Modern Fiction Studies* 25 (1979): 407. Johnson

concludes that Mr. R. is "an ego-alphabetic surrogate of Vladimir Nabokov" (p. 408).

3. See, for example, Gleb Struve, "Nabokov as a Russian Writer," in *Nabokov*, ed. Dembo, p. 54: "What makes Nabokov even more alien to the Russian literary tradition is his lack of sympathy with, if not interest in, human beings as such"; Brown, "Nabokov's Pushkin," in *Nabokov*, ed. Dembo, p. 208: "The only fate with which Nabokov has ever been in the least concerned [is] the fate of art itself."

4. Ellen Pifer makes a similar observation about the moral implications of Humbert Humbert's murder of Quilty: "In my opinion, the only artist justified in killing off Quilty for the sake of art (and the artful narration) is his creator, Nabokov. The author of the artifice reserves the right to dictate the course of events in the private world of his creation. *Within* the fictional framework, however, the murder of one character by another may not be so lightly dismissed." See *Nabokov and the Novel*, p. 108.

5. For a useful discussion of the coincidences and patterns of details in the novel, especially the details associated with murder and fire, see de Jonge, "Nabokov's Uses of Pattern," in *Vladimir Nabokov*, ed. Quennell, pp. 59–72.

6. "Restoration," in *Poems and Problems*, p. 167.

Chapter VIII

1. William Butler Yeats, *The Collected Poems of W. B. Yeats* (New York: Macmillan, 1973), pp. 335–36.

2. I am not the first to hear echoes of "The Circus Animals' Desertion" in Nabokov's novel. Richard Patteson has also noticed the similarity, although he uses the comparison for purposes very different from my own. See "Nabokov's *Look at the Harlequins!*: Endless Re-Creation of the Self," *Russian Literature Triquarterly* 14 (1976): 84–98.

3. Compare Robert Merrill's comment, "Imagine Vladimir Nabokov writing in praise of 'ordinariness'!" in "Nabokov and Fictional Artifices," *Modern Fiction Studies* 25 (1979): 442. The most extensive discussions of the theme of art in Nabokov's fiction can be found in Bader's *Crystal Land*, Stegner's *Escape into Aesthetics*, and, not surprisingly, in Nabokov's *Strong Opinions*. For an intelligent rebuttal to those critics who argue that Nabokov's chief interest is in the creative act itself, see Pifer, *Nabokov and the Novel*. Pifer attempts to qualify what she sees as the prevailing opinion that Nabokov is "an aesthete indifferent to the everyday struggles of humanity—an art-

ist in perpetual flight from the sordid realities of this world, soaring like Icarus into the realm of 'aesthetic bliss'" (pp. 1–2).

4. Grabes finds another definitive difference between Nabokov and Vadim Vadimovich; he concludes, inexplicably, that Vadim dies— literally—"in the final incompleted sentence of the book." See *Fictitious Biographies*, p. 106.

5. Jonathan Raban, review of *Look at the Harlequins!*, *Encounter*, June 1975, p. 81; John Updike, review of *Look at the Harlequins!*, *New Yorker*, November 11, 1974, p. 209.

6. There is evidence that Nabokov had some firsthand experience with the art of pantomime. During his early years in Berlin he worked as a writer for the Blue Bird Theater, a cabaret that entertained customers with brief dramatic skits. In a letter written to his mother during this period Nabokov refers to one of his scripts for the Blue Bird as a "pantomime." See Andrew Field, *Nabokov: His Life in Part* (New York: Viking Press, 1977), pp. 162, 174.

7. Compare Nabokov's remarks about his own early poetry: "The kind of poem I produced in those days was hardly anything more than a sign I made of being alive, of passing or having passed, or hoping to pass, through certain intense human emotions" (*Speak, Memory*, p. 217).

8. *Glory*, p. xiii. Nabokov's comment includes a rebuke apparently directed at Page Stegner, author of *Escape into Aesthetics*.

9. *W. B. Yeats and T. Sturge Moore: Their Correspondence, 1901–1937*, ed. Ursula Bridge (New York: Oxford University Press, 1953), p. 154.

Index